AF326559

God Is My Ghostwriter

GOD
IS MY
GHOSTWRITER

Letting Go, Tuning In, and
Creating the Life You Were Meant to Live

DANIELLE K. WHITE

GOD IS MY GHOSTWRITER

Letting Go, Tuning In, and Creating the Life You Were Meant to Live

FIRST EDITION

ISBN   978-1-5445-5179-1 *Hardcover*

       978-1-5445-5178-4 *Paperback*

       978-1-5445-5180-7 *Ebook*

CONTENTS

INTRODUCTION

I WAS EIGHT MONTHS PREGNANT WITH MY SECOND daughter when my husband confessed that he was having an emotional affair.

It was 2011, and I thought we'd hit rock bottom already. Our cars had been repossessed. We had short-sold our home. We were hundreds of thousands in debt. So I didn't think anything of Garrett coming home at 10:00 p.m.—he often worked late trying to provide for our family.

That night, Garrett came straight to the living room, where I'd been watching TV, and sat across from me. He seemed nervous. Before I could ask what his deal was, he admitted to kissing his client, a woman who also happened to be my sister's friend.

Ew, I immediately thought, more disgusted than angry. I don't remember what I thought or said next, but eventually I asked what I considered the most important question: "Did you have sex with her?"

"No," he replied.

"Okay, so how did this happen?"

Garrett and I were both raised Mormon, so cheating was never an option in my mind. Frankly, he seemed shocked by what he'd done as well. But as he explained how they'd just locked eyes and leaned in—and that it wouldn't happen again—I felt myself growing numb. *Has he done this before? Is it going to go further? Where are we at?*

Over the following weeks, as I prepared for and gave birth to our second daughter, Garrett's guilt prompted him to spill more details. He and his client often had lunch together. They went on hikes. Held hands. They had basically been dating for three months. We weren't connecting as husband and wife, so he had been getting his emotional needs met elsewhere.

Listen, asshole, I thought, *I am freaking pregnant!*

Many women, especially those from traditional cultures, seek safety and security in their husbands. So now that Garrett and I had lost everything, including trust, I wondered about leaving. Could I provide for my daughters as a hairstylist? Fear and hurt were telling me to call it quits, but I couldn't say that I'd done my best in the relationship either.

Though I resented my husband for putting us in this situation, I decided I owed it to the girls to try to heal our broken communication patterns, to rekindle the fiery chemistry we'd once had. Or, if that failed, to figure out how I could be successful as a single mom.

Of course, in the meantime, I wasn't going to tell anyone that Garrett had an affair. Doing so would be scary, embarrassing. So I told myself that I'd shut my mouth and work on myself and our marriage alone, in secret.

That's when I heard a voice that I'd ignored since my teenage years say, *No. That's not what you're supposed to do.*

And for the first time, I responded: *Okay, so what does that mean?*

When you're totally exposed, you have no choice but to be honest with yourself. It was only then, after the life my husband and I had built was stripped away piece by piece, that I realized I wasn't happy. And neither was Garrett. We did all the "right" things according to our culture's rules (e.g., getting married in the temple, allowing the husband to provide), but we were both miserable.

I know grown adults who hide their drinking from their seventy-year-old parents, who stay in abusive relationships for the kids. Even after realizing they're miserable, a lot of people remain in situations that don't serve them because they start wondering, *What is my mom going to think? What will my friends say?* Maybe that's where you're at right now.

It's true that there will be backlash. People won't get it when you do something different. They'll project their fears onto you and call it concern. But finding the courage to get outside your comfort zone is when you'll finally start feeling free. That's when you'll begin to succeed in ways they never thought possible.

In the fallout of Garrett's emotional affair, I understood at last that I wasn't meant to follow someone else's path—I was meant to forge my own. To me, intuition like this comes from God, and I've since recognized His writing in all the pivotal moments of my life—especially when the best decisions for me were not the ones that made sense to others.

Once I started trusting my intuition, I was able to let go of the limiting beliefs that held me back in every area of my life. I repaired my marriage and built a successful hair extensions and education business, Natural Beaded Rows (NBR). I designed online courses and in-person trainings, hosted events with hundreds of attendees, and created the podcasts *Date Your Wife* and *The Danielle K. White Show*. I bought a multimillion-dollar dream home and welcomed two more beautiful girls into the world. And

I'm not settling now, knowing there's more I can do for my family and the community I've built.

Before you read on, consider, do you lack purpose? Do you feel caged by the expectations of your industry, your religion, marriage, parenthood, or any other social construct? Do you long for something more but not know where to begin?

If so, trust me, I've been there. That's why I kept hearing God tell me to share my story—not to give specific religious, business, or self-development advice but to empower and encourage others who feel stuck. I genuinely believe that we're here to serve, and the more we listen to our intuition, the more opportunities we'll have to do so.

With innovation and integrity, anyone can build the life of their dreams, but it doesn't happen overnight. So let's rewind twenty years...all the way back to when I was first getting on this roller coaster with the man who would become my husband.

Chapter 1

BREAKING CULTURAL NORMS

ONE AFTERNOON, WHEN I WAS EIGHTEEN AND LIVING on my own for the first time, in Orem, Utah, a girl I only vaguely knew from my apartment complex came over to hang out with my roommates. Despite our limited familiarity, as soon as I opened the door, she said, "So, I heard you're dating Garrett White."

Just a few weeks prior, I'd decided to go to a Mormon fireside with thousands of students from Utah Valley University, even though I'd spent the summer drinking beer and dating creepy guys instead of attending church. I was hoping to make some friends, but instead I met Garrett.

At the time, Garrett had earrings, spiky hair with frosted tips, and a "tribal" tattoo around his bicep that looked more like the logo for the Boy Scouts of America (the result of a drunken night with his college football buddies). He seemed wild compared to the clean-shaven Mormon men I grew up with. Like a rebel. But as someone who'd always felt like a black sheep, who didn't understand why I had to abide by rules like going to seminary before school every day, I found myself drawn to him.

Before I knew it, we were talking like I'd never talked with anyone else, connecting in a way I'd never connected with my summer flings or even my high school boyfriend. Garrett was seven years older than me, yet it felt like our vibrations were in the same place.

Smiling at the memory, I told the girl in my apartment, "Yeah, I am."

"That's so awesome!" she said, which was surprising given the judgment we typically received because of our age gap. "Ask him about his son."

I was confused. Garrett hadn't mentioned a kid, and when would he have even had one? Like most Mormon men, and some women, he'd gone on a mission for two years after graduating high school.

"Oh, no," I responded. "Must be a different Garrett White."

The girl shook her head. "You know, Garrett White? Lives in 303? He has a son who's really cute."

Did she date him? How does she know?

"Huh, that's...interesting," I said, wondering how on earth I was going to bring the subject up when I saw him that evening.

At that point, I'd kissed Garrett, but our relationship was still fresh. All I could think was that I wouldn't have started seeing him if I'd known he was a *father*. I was barely an adult, after all.

A few hours later, I went to Garret's apartment and sat on his couch as he cooked dinner. Knowing there was no easy way to ask about his son, I simply told him about my encounter with the girl in our complex. To my surprise, his response was completely nonchalant. "Yeah, I do. There's a picture of him in my room."

I flushed. I'd seen that framed picture before but had assumed the adorable little boy in a baseball cap was Garrett's nephew. I'd thought it was sweet that he had such a strong relationship with him.

I ran to the other room and came back holding the picture. "This is your son?"

"Yeah."

"How old is he?"

"Two."

Garrett brought the food he'd made over, and I began peppering him with questions. Apparently, he hadn't just knocked someone up; he met a girl and married her within six months of returning from his mission. He was twenty-one and she was eighteen, but that wasn't even uncommon in Boise because pre-marital sex is so taboo in the Mormon culture.

Garrett and his ex fought all the time—so much so that they almost called off the wedding the day before. But they ultimately went through with it because of cultural pressure. Three months later, she was pregnant.

I don't typically let people see my emotions, so on the outside, I maintained a collected demeanor and kept prying. Inside, though, I was panicking. *How do I get out? Should I just run out of the apartment right now? That might be weird. He might think I'm weird. But I can't keep dating him—not only is he seven years older, but he has a kid! What will everyone think?*

Oblivious to my inner hurricane, Garrett went on to tell me that his son had been born in Idaho, but they soon moved to Canada to be closer to his ex's family. Garrett had to let go of his football scholarship to make the move, but even in another country, even with a child, he and his ex kept fighting. So, when Parker was six months old, he chose to leave. Now he only saw his son, Parker, a couple of times each year.

At eighteen, hearing that was a relief. I wasn't sure that I wanted kids at that point in my life or that our relationship was going anywhere. I certainly wasn't ready to be a stepmom. I just wanted to have fun with Garrett, to hang out and make out, not babysit a toddler.

News travels fast in the tight-knit Mormon community, and it wasn't long before I received a call from my mom that began, "So, I heard you're dating somebody."

Though I still had reservations about our relationship, Garrett and I were now exclusive, so I said, "Yeah, you'd really like him."

"I heard he's twenty-five and has a kid."

"Yeah."

There was a pause, and then she said, "Well, there are a lot of fish in the sea."

I laughed. "Don't worry; it's not that serious. We're just having fun."

But Garrett and I kept dating, and around the three-month mark, my mom called again. "It seems like you really like this guy. We'd love to meet him."

The next thing I knew, I was waiting anxiously at my parents' ten-thousand-square-foot home for Garrett to roll up in his newly bought Honda Prelude. On our first date, he'd picked me up in his friend's truck instead of his $500 piece-of-shit vehicle because he knew I had a nice car. The Prelude was his first big purchase since starting in mortgages—and the first indication I saw that he was a hard worker, one who could meet the standards I'd been raised with.

Not that my parents would care what kind of car Garrett drove. My dad is a salt-of-the-earth cowboy, a stocky, six-foot construction worker who wears the same T-shirt and jeans every day. He seems intimidating but is not-so-secretly a teddy bear. My mom, meanwhile, is a real estate agent who loves nice things and dressing cute. She can seem judgmental, but once you get through her tough exterior, she takes you as her blood.

My parents were at the height of their careers when Garrett met them in 2002, but they were and still are down-to-earth people. So imagine my surprise when my boyfriend arrived and stepped out of his new car in a suit, looking nervous for the first time since I'd met him. *Here he comes*, I thought, both amused and touched.

My dad opened the front door and held it as Garrett strolled over and shook his hand. Then, without preamble, he asked, "Why do you like my daughter?"

Garrett stammered something about how I was beautiful and funny until my dad had mercy and patted him on the back. "You seem like a nice guy," he said before walking off.

These days, my parents, my sister, and I hug and say "I love you" whenever we see each other, but when I was growing up, we were close but didn't show affection much. We mostly kept to ourselves. So it was another surprise when my mom came over and immediately embraced Garrett, welcoming him like he was already family.

The rest of that visit is a blur, but Garrett got along great with my parents. He wasn't the kind of person they expected me to date, but before long, I was convinced they liked him more than they liked me. But maybe they just liked that this loud giant got their quiet, petite daughter to open up. And maybe they could already tell that God was writing him into my story despite our vastly different personalities and—I was soon to learn—backgrounds.

On Christmas Eve, Garrett and I drove to Brigham City, a tiny town about an hour outside of Salt Lake, and parked in front of a house that looked like it had just been plopped onto a random lot. I looked around, brow furrowed, and asked, "What is this?"

Garrett explained that his family's home had been manufactured elsewhere and delivered there rather than being built directly on the land. It was basically a step above a trailer. He said all this casually, but I could tell he felt embarrassed after seeing how I was raised.

I don't remember thinking much about that information, especially since I was soon overwhelmed by attention from Garrett's parents and siblings. *My god, do I have to hug everybody?* I wondered as yet another person gave me a tight squeeze. As I've said, physical affection wasn't the norm for me back then—and the noise definitely wasn't either. But they were all thrilled that Garrett had come home with a new car and a cute girl; they felt like he'd "made it."

A little while later, before I'd really had a chance to settle in, I was caught off guard again. "All right," someone said, "I think it's time to head on down to Walmart."

"What?" I asked Garrett.

He told me then that it was his family's tradition to buy each other gifts at Walmart on Christmas Eve. I couldn't believe it. They didn't purchase gifts beforehand? And Brigham City didn't even have a Target?

"Nope," Garrett said as he led me back out of the house, "just some fast food and Walmart."

In the yard, his siblings were piling into the back of a pickup truck stuffed with hay barrels. *What the hell?* I thought, but Garrett didn't seem to find this strange. He and I climbed in too, and then his dad took off down a dirt road. (I learned later that there was a *paved* road to the local superstore, but his parents didn't want to get stopped for having people in the truck bed.)

Since Garrett now had money, he decided to treat his whole family to matching blue sweaters. Later, when we returned from Walmart, I helped him wrap them. The whole experience was surreal but fun, and I was struck by how at ease we felt in each other's family homes despite their differences.

That night, for the first time, Garrett told me he loved me.

As someone who doesn't easily or quickly share feelings, I felt a bit uncomfortable, but I said the words back. It was Christmas Eve, after all, and the whole night had felt like a Hallmark movie.

In the spring, Garrett broke up with me, saying that I should date other people, that I was too smart and pretty and young to be seeing someone like him, that he wasn't letting me fully experience college life, never mind that I was actually in hair school.

So I'd go on dates, and he'd get jealous. We'd see each other again, and I'd think, *Okay, cool, because I really just want to be with you.* Then he'd break up with me again, and I'd just want him more. This happened four or five times.

I think Garrett felt unworthy of a connection like ours because he was older and had been married, but I liked that he was established, that he didn't mess around. In the short period we'd been together, I'd seen him go from making no money as a server to making over $10,000/month as a loan officer. I could tell that he'd be successful no matter what he did and that drive was almost as attractive to me as his appearance and personality.

By my community's standards, our relationship didn't make sense. If you'd shown me Garrett when I was in high school and said he was the man I'd marry, I would've replied, "No, he's not." He just didn't fit the mold. But even back then, my intuition told me that I wasn't meant to be with the picture-perfect Mormon man. That's ultimately why I didn't marry my high school boyfriend of two years (well, that and the fact that we had no chemistry).

But while it felt like all my friends were on the hunt for husbands, I wasn't ready to marry Garrett. Even after we started talking about getting engaged, I wasn't opposed to dating for a few years and moving in together first. I didn't care about breaking my culture's norms, only that I wasn't reduced to the stereotypical nineteen-year-old wife and mom.

In what I think was a final test to see if I really wanted to be with him, Garrett invited me on his twelve-hour road trip to Canada so that I could meet his ex-wife and son. And to our surprise, it was a lovely time. Garrett's ex was sweet and energetic, someone I thought I could hang out with, and Parker was an absolute delight. I loved spending the week taking him to the mall and water park.

By the time we were heading home, I no longer thought of Parker as someone I'd have to deal with on occasion if I married Garrett. I was excited to have him be a part of our family. Not only that, but I was also excited to have my own children. For the first time, I knew I wanted to be a mom.

Plus, that trip apparently convinced Garrett I was his woman. He stopped breaking up with me and instead took me to my aunt and uncle's jewelry shop. I picked out a ring, no longer scared of getting engaged.

Even though I'd never wanted to get married young, I knew that I wanted to be with Garrett. We had such an amazing connection, and he was ready to remarry. I was ready for him to stop pushing me away. In my mind, a ring signified security.

One afternoon, when I was nineteen and honing my haircutting skills, the school's receptionist called me to the front of the salon. Thinking I had a new client, I hurried over and saw two of Garrett's friends. They were dressed in black suits and ties and wearing sunglasses like they were the Men in Black.

"Ma'am, you need to come with us," one of them said, as if they were going to arrest me.

Ever since we'd looked at rings, I'd been expecting Garrett to propose, but being naturally introverted, I didn't expect *this*. I could practically feel the other hundred students craning their necks to look at me. I shouldn't have been surprised, though; everything Garrett does is grandiose.

I followed his friends outside to a limo, where some guy sat inside with a video camera, filming. We then drove to my apartment, and I was told that I had thirty minutes to freshen up before they retrieved me for dinner.

In my apartment, I found rose petals strewn across the hallway, all the way into my bedroom. On my bed were more petals, as well as a super cute black dress and strappy black heels. It was all so well executed that I felt overwhelmed with love.

After I was ready, Garrett's friends took me to La Caille, a prestigious restaurant in the Salt Lake area where many people have their wedding receptions. Standing outside, wearing a rented tux, was my boyfriend. If I had any doubt that he would propose that night, it was erased seeing him dressed to the nines like that.

After we ate dinner, Garrett led me onto a dance floor. We swayed to the music for a few minutes, and then he brought me to a fountain and gestured to the bottom. Under the water, in pennies, I saw that he'd spelled out "Will you marry me?" When I turned back toward him, he got down on his knee and asked out loud.

One of the sweetest things about Garrett is that he always wants to meet the standards that he thinks I expect, and he unquestionably exceeded them with his proposal. The whole night was so much more thoughtful and romantic than I could've imagined.

The next day, I went back to my hair school wearing a ring with a carat-and-a-half diamond—fairly large for a nineteen-year-old, especially in a small town. The girls *oohed* and *aahed*, and one even asked, "Oh my god, are you marrying Donald Trump?" which is funny in retrospect because he wasn't president at the time, just some rich guy.

"I don't know. Maybe," I joked.

Despite how young I was, everyone I knew was supportive of our engagement; they didn't think it was weird at all. In the Mormon culture, it's not unusual to get engaged within six months and married two months after that, so it actually surprised people that we'd dated for almost a year and were planning on getting married in another six months. My roommates, for instance, couldn't wait to fall in love, have a fairy-tale wedding, pump out babies, and live happily ever after.

That's the path we were all taught to follow. But I've never been great with directions.

Chapter 2

LIVING THE FAIRY TALE

GARRETT AND I HAD A TRADITIONAL BUT NOT PARTICU-larly memorable wedding in a Mormon temple shortly after I turned twenty. Even then, I felt like the ceremony didn't resonate with me, but we went through with it to appease our parents. I didn't really question it, because of the culture we were raised in; it was just another item on the devout Mormon checklist.

Six months into our marriage, Garrett announced that we were moving to Nevada. Business was booming in Las Vegas, and he and a coworker wanted to capitalize on it by building their own mortgage company.

"No," I said. "I'm not moving away from my family."

For several days, every time Garrett brought moving up, I shut the conversation down. Since our wedding, we'd been abiding by our community's standards. No more drinking. No more skipping church. No one left the Utah bubble—they raised their families in the areas they were raised in—so we wouldn't leave either. It didn't even occur to me to question, let alone look beyond, the box I was raised in.

I finally began to entertain the idea when Garrett said he'd buy me a house in Vegas. We'd been living in a shithole apartment next to a prison, listening to the couple above us screaming and throwing things at each other, because my husband had been raised in scarcity. He was making good money, but early in our marriage, he found even townhome prices ludicrously expensive. So I jumped on the offer of home ownership, and we flew to Vegas.

During our visit, we toured a few different homes in Green Valley Ranch, a cute neighborhood that a Realtor friend recommended, but there was one that I fell in love with the minute we walked through the front door. It was 3,500 square feet—gigantic compared to our apartment—and had a pool and hot tub. Standing in the threshold, I envisioned myself cruising down Las Vegas Boulevard in the Audi TT convertible Garrett had bought me the previous Christmas, on my way back to the immaculately decorated house we now called home.

The decision to move might not have made sense to our community, but at that moment, it felt right to me. We put in an offer, which was quickly accepted, and soon we were young newlyweds ready to begin our fairy tale in a new state.

Being outside the Utah bubble *was* fun at first. Garrett and I enjoyed finding cool restaurants to try, and we were less tuned in to the gossip that pervades small communities. But the pressure of starting a company meant that Garrett was soon working until 9:00 or 10:00 p.m. most nights.

When we were dating, he would often work late, but when you're college-aged, that seems normal. You often don't have dinner until 9:00 p.m. anyway. Yet as a wife, I wanted the typical married lifestyle, not to go to the gym and watch movies alone. My husband took off Sundays just so we could go to church, and

I felt that I couldn't complain since I didn't want to give up our nice house and cars.

To pass my time, I began working on commission at a nice salon in town, but I was so anxious about messing up that I felt nauseous driving to work every day. I couldn't believe people would trust me—someone who'd only recently finished hair school—with coloring and cuts and extensions. For months, I had to force myself to get out of bed and go, but I found that I had a knack for doing hair. And I eventually became more comfortable chatting with clients.

One of the reasons I'd decided to go to hair school in the first place was that I wanted to learn extensions. I'd never been able to grow out my fine hair and always felt self-conscious about the way it looked, but it turns out you don't learn extensions in hair school. So I completed multiple certifications trying to find a solution for myself, and then I started mixing techniques.

At the time, tape-in and fusion extensions were all the rage, but I found that the thinner hand-tied hair—sold all the way at the back of beauty stores—was more cost-effective. If I stacked multiple wefts on a single row, I could achieve the same full look with fewer places where the hair was attached to the scalp. This made the process faster for me, and it seemed like a healthier solution for my clients.

Little did I know that my innovative technique would someday lead to hand-tied hair skyrocketing in popularity. For the moment, I was simply pleased that I had solved my own hair struggles and quickly had a solid book of business. Within a year, even the salon's owner was asking me to do her hair extensions.

Between the cost-effective hair, my more efficient technique, and my growing client base, I started making good money for the first time in my life. It was a hectic period, but because Garrett was always working, I didn't feel the need to cut back. I did, however, decide to split the rent on a booth in a fancier salon with another hairstylist. I didn't know if any of my clients would follow me there, but I was tired of working on commission.

Fortunately, most of my clients did follow me. Before long, I could work four days per week and still make upward of $10,000 per month.

What's crazy is that I was just stockpiling all this money. As newlyweds, Garrett and I had separate bank accounts, and having grown up in the patriarchal Mormon culture, I expected him to pay the bills out of his. I was only working because I enjoyed it.

Garrett was the provider, not me. And, I told him, I never would be.

As our businesses grew, Garrett and I basically stopped dating. We'd still have dinner together a couple of nights each week, but we weren't having deep conversations. We weren't going on drives because we liked being together or talking for hours on the phone because we wanted to hear each other's voice. I assumed that's just how it is when you're married; you both hustle and grind, and maybe after ten years and two kids, you'll be established enough that you can take the time to connect again.

Often when it was late and I was in the middle of watching *House Hunters*, Garrett would come home, exhausted, and ask me to go to bed with him. I'd tell him that I was finishing my show and wasn't tired, but we both knew that he was really saying, *Okay, I did my job. Now you need to come upstairs and have sex.* And I'd think, *You didn't hang out with me. You didn't even say hi to me.*

Every once in a while, I'd throw Garrett a bone just to avoid an argument, but that was the problem. Sex felt like an obligation. I couldn't figure out why I wasn't attracted to my husband, why I just felt numb.

What's wrong with me? I wondered. *Am I broken?*

I've since learned that this experience is common for women, especially those who grew up repressing their sexuality. We lose all sexual desire when we feel disconnected from our husbands, and then our husbands feel sexually frustrated. We feel like we can't talk about the issue with anyone because it's taboo to air your dirty laundry, so the vicious cycle continues. Resentment builds, and we blame ourselves.

The disconnect between me and Garrett came to a head on my twenty-first birthday. That morning, I started making breakfast, and he didn't say anything. I got ready for work, and he didn't say anything.

This asshole has forgotten my birthday, I thought. Then I chose to be optimistic. *No, surely he's got something planned for tonight.*

I went to the salon and tried not to think about Garrett, but he wasn't home when I returned. He finally walked in around 8:00 p.m. while I was sitting at the kitchen table, eating a chicken sandwich that I'd made. I was pissed as hell.

"Hey, what are you doing?" Garrett asked, still oblivious.

I glared at him. "Today's my birthday."

His eyes widened in panic. "Wait, what?"

"You forgot my twenty-first birthday."

Garrett immediately tried to backpedal. "No, I definitely have something planned. I was going to save it for this weekend."

I didn't really believe him, but I was too tired to be mad anymore. I stood up and started heading toward the stairs, ready for bed. "Okay, I guess we'll do something this weekend," I said.

To Garrett's credit, when I came home from the salon the next day, there was a birthday banner hanging up and wiener dogs running down the hall. We had recently gotten Lizzy, a two-pound puppy, at a strip mall and hadn't discussed getting another dog, but Cloey was so cute that I completely forgave my husband. For a moment, she fixed everything.

Of course, the peace didn't last, because Garrett and I didn't address the reasons behind our growing resentment. Neither of us even acknowledged that we'd spent our entire time in Vegas creating bad habits and unhealthy communication patterns. So, in retrospect, it's not surprising that we had our first blowup fight only a couple of months after my birthday.

I don't remember now what that fight was about, but I remember tossing and turning in one of the guest beds all night, thinking, *I'm done. I'm going to divorce him.*

Then my intuition interrupted that train of thought. *If you think this is going to be any different with another husband, you're wrong. You'll just create a whole new set of problems with somebody else if you don't figure out what's going on with you.*

I see now that God was nudging me in the right direction, but at twenty-one, I had no idea how to self-reflect. All I knew was that I was lonely. Not only were Garrett and I basically glorified roommates, but we were also physically separated from our families. We didn't even get to see Parker during this period because Garrett and his ex were fighting over child support. Meanwhile, one by one, my friends were crossing off the next item on the Mormon checklist: become a mom.

Not knowing any better, I started to think that having a child would heal the void inside me, so I applied myself to baby-making with the intensity that I had given to expanding my hair business. Yet after nine months, I still wasn't pregnant.

Why is this taking so long? I wondered, frustrated. I didn't even enjoy sex, and it felt like we were having it all the time now.

"You have to have sex when you're ovulating," my older sister said when I finally mustered up the courage to ask her what to do. She was incredulous that no one had explained the process to me. "Go to the store and buy an ovulation kit."

So I did, and soon enough I was expecting. Garrett and I were both ecstatic. I was only nine weeks along, but we told everyone we knew—our families, our church, our coworkers—and they were all excited for us. It felt like maybe everything would be okay.

Then one evening while getting ready to go to a movie, I suddenly felt wet, like I'd just peed my pants. I rushed to the bathroom and saw a ton of blood, so I called my doctor. He told me I needed to get to the hospital.

Garrett drove me there, and the doctor checked me out. He said that I was miscarrying and needed a D&C (dilation and curettage), a procedure used to remove uterine tissue. I nodded and underwent the procedure, and the next day, I was discharged as if nothing had happened.

I couldn't believe it. We hadn't even heard the baby's heartbeat, and now they were gone.

The trauma of that first pregnancy was hard on both me and Garrett, especially when well-meaning people at church would congratulate us and we'd have to explain that we lost our child. We wanted to try again as soon as I safely could, but that didn't mean we weren't grieving.

I'd been thinking for a while that I wanted to return to Utah—Vegas was so expensive that we could get a house twice as big back home—but the miscarriage was really the catalyst for our move. I found that I wanted to be surrounded by family and friends when I got pregnant again. I figured maybe there was a reason all the people I grew up with stayed within a ten-mile radius of their childhood homes.

The thing is, whether we're Mormon or atheist, present on every social platform or completely off the grid, we all learn a fixed set of rules, and we're taught not to question them. Yet too often we do everything we're expected to do only to realize we're not happy. We're not actually listening to our hearts, our God, whatever you want to call it. And when we repeatedly ignore that little voice, tuning in to it becomes harder.

At twenty-two, I followed one rule down to the letter: don't complain about your life. Don't complain about your miscarriage, and certainly don't complain about your husband. Because if you're not grateful, everything you care about might be taken away. More pressing, others will judge you for *being* ungrateful.

So I didn't complain. And since I had nothing to complain about, nothing had to change.

Chapter 3

IGNORING THE SIGNS

WITHIN SIX MONTHS OF MOVING TO SANDY, UTAH, GARRETT and I were expecting again. We had a seven-thousand-square-foot home, I'd upgraded my Audi to a Range Rover, and life seemed blessed. I thought we'd made it.

But unlike other women in my community, I didn't enjoy being pregnant. I didn't have morning sickness, but I had so much brain fog that my days blurred together. I wasn't doing hair, so I had nothing to occupy those days besides settling into our new home. I gained sixty pounds, which was a lot on my petite frame, so I didn't feel cute when I left our home in my carefully curated outfits. Overall, I didn't feel like I was glowing; I didn't even feel like I was in my own body. I felt like a zombie—and experienced prenatal mom guilt because of it.

Meanwhile, work wasn't slowing down for Garrett. Not only was he running his own mortgage company, but he was also being asked to speak at real estate conventions. These conventions didn't pay him, and they didn't really help his career, but they made him feel significant. So he went.

I started to resent the time Garrett spent away from home, but again, I grew up with the traditional mindset that the husband is supposed to provide. Since I expected him to provide us with a grand lifestyle, I had to accept that he would work long hours. I couldn't ask for more of his time.

This will all get better once I have the baby, I thought.

I didn't realize then that money can be a mask. When you're busy "having fun" at fancy dinners and on lavish vacations, no one can tell that you and your partner have issues. Or, at least, no one acknowledges them. Not even you.

I was a couple of days overdue when I went into labor with my first daughter, but Bailee still took her sweet time getting here. After Garrett rushed me to the hospital, I spent twenty hours throwing up on and off, alternately sick from the epidural and sick from the pain.

By the time my doctor suggested that I undergo an emergency C-section, I was adamant about having a natural birth. I'd already spent a full day laboring, dammit, and they couldn't give me any more drugs. My whole body was screaming.

"We'll have to use the vacuum, then," he told me.

"Okay, fine."

The next thing I knew, two nurses were pushing my stomach, and the doctor was suctioning my baby's head. Moments later, Bailee finally popped out. I was so relieved, I couldn't speak.

A nurse handed my beautiful baby girl to me, and I was surprised to see that she wasn't even crying. She just looked around the room, like she was also in shock from the trauma of her birth.

Gosh, I thought, *she's so alert.*

Later, when I took off Bailee's beanie, I saw that her head was cone-shaped and there was a ring around it from the vacuum. But she was healthy, nearly nine pounds and with strong vitals, and that was enough. Everyone assured me her head would look normal soon.

Breastfeeding was anything but normal, though. In the hospital, I couldn't get Bailee to latch well, even with the nurses' help. After we were discharged, I often experienced clogged ducts and cracked nipples. For four months, I dreaded nursing my baby, all while my friends went on and on about how much they loved that particular bonding experience.

As a wife, it was my job to get up in the night to change and feed Bailee. Garrett needed his sleep for work, and he was still traveling half the time anyway. So now I was up crying from the pain and guilt of struggling to nurse, and yet my baby clearly wasn't getting all the nutrients she needed.

It got so bad that I decided to talk to a lactation specialist about introducing a bit of formula, but she made me feel awful for even considering it, like I was deficient as a mother. In one conversation, she confirmed what I feared all those sleepless nights: that I was broken.

I didn't tell Garrett about that visit. I didn't ask him for help, let alone admit that I was exhausted and defeated. In my mind, taking care of our daughter was my responsibility, just as providing for our family was his.

Interestingly, it was at the six-month mark, when I chose to ignore the lactation consultant's recommendation and start integrating formula into Bailee's diet, that motherhood changed for me. Once my daughter was getting enough food, we both began sleeping through the night. My hormones became regulated, and I dropped the rest of the pregnancy weight. I resumed going to the gym and lunch dates with friends, happy to show my precious baby off to anyone and everyone.

At last I felt human again.

As much as I loved being a mom, I needed a creative outlet. I knew, deep down, that staying home all day was part of the reason I didn't feel like myself when Bailee was an infant. So I decided to start rebuilding my book of clients.

For about a year and a half, after Bailee turned two and I put her in a daycare, I rented a chair a few days per week at a salon that my older sister worked at. I used the extensions technique that I had developed in Las Vegas and even taught it to my sister and sister-in-law, if only so we could do each other's hair.

With the cost of daycare, I was barely breaking even, but I didn't raise my prices. I was only doing hair for fun. I saw any extra income I brought home as hobby money since Garrett was in charge of making ends meet.

Even then, I could tell that he was stressed. With the house and cars and baby, our expenses had doubled over the past couple of years, and he'd compensated by scaling his business from twenty employees to nearly one hundred. But I didn't know how to help relieve his stress; neither of us knew how to identify or communicate what we needed from each other.

Garrett's desire for connection usually manifested as a request for sex. Every week or so, I'd put out, but I had no interest in being intimate with my husband. I didn't even realize my lack of interest was a result of our disconnect. I didn't care enough to analyze it.

Four years into our marriage, Garrett and I were simply coexisting. In the Mormon community, the husband works and the wife cares for the family; spouses don't waste money on going out, on maintaining a connection. So I didn't think anything of the fact that I hardly saw him, that we weren't talking.

At the time, the only thing I really pushed for was seeing Parker at least twice a year. I wanted Bailee to know her half brother, and I knew Garrett would regret it later if he didn't have a relationship with his son. As long as we were financially stable, all I cared about was being the best mom and stepmom I could be.

The problem is that it was 2009, and the market downturn was catching up to us. I just didn't know it yet.

Early on, Garrett and I put both personal and business expenses on credit so that we could earn points. I was used to paying off thousands at a time on our Visa and American Express cards. But one night when I logged on to our (now shared) bank account, I saw that we owed $40,000 on a single card.

Does he know what he's doing? I wondered while paying as much on the card as we could comfortably afford. Then I reminded myself, *He's the provider. I'm sure he knows what he's doing.*

Month after month, I tried to maintain that optimism, but our credit card debt kept exponentially increasing, so I knew we weren't bringing home enough money. Before long, we owed $100,000 across multiple cards, yet our lifestyle didn't change. In fact, Garrett hired a tailor to make custom suits so his hundred employees could come into the office dressed to the nines.

I couldn't believe it. We weren't paying off our credit cards, and now my husband was blowing more money on suits? Who the fuck was this guy?

Throughout the COVID-19 pandemic, I saw entrepreneurs lose their businesses because they didn't know how to pivot or because they were worried about maintaining their image. By 2020, Garrett and I understood what it meant to make business decisions that align with your true purpose, not some societal ideal, but we had no idea what to do during the recession.

For longer than I care to admit, my intuition screamed at me to do something, say something, but I ignored it. I willfully ignored all the signs that things were going seriously wrong. Because of how I was raised, I told myself that Garrett was responsible for our situation. That he would take care of us. I defaulted to my husband's judgment even though I saw that he was simply defaulting to what he'd seen others do.

Still, I couldn't stay silent forever. One night in the kitchen, I decided to confront Garrett, credit card statement in hand. "Hey, babe," I began, "you should probably let go of some of your team members."

"What?" he asked, genuinely surprised. "I'm not worried about it. I'll pay it all back."

Over the course of several weeks, we had many of these conversations. I'd prod Garrett about our deteriorating financial situation, and he'd brush off my concerns as if I couldn't see the debts racking up. Too soon, we'd maxed out all our credit cards and owed nearly half a million dollars in total.

What are we going to do? I thought, panic seeping in one evening as I checked our balances. *How will we ever get out of this?*

Those questions kept haunting me, to the point where I felt betrayed by my husband, repulsed whenever he was around. It was his job to take care of us, after all.

"Why are you still employing your mom?" I eventually demanded. "Why aren't you firing your brother? You're paying him $10,000 a month, and we're not even paying our own bills!"

Garrett was angry. "Things will turn around. You just need to trust me."

But I didn't. I was scared, and I could tell by the look in his eyes that he was too.

Chapter 4

HITTING ROCK BOTTOM

WHEN OUR DEBT BECAME SO UNMANAGEABLE THAT WE stopped making regular payments, my Range Rover was repossessed, and Garrett sold his Lincoln Navigator. Instead of filing for bankruptcy, we short-sold our home and rented a house from someone who was also struggling to pay their mortgage. Our credit was so shot that my mom cosigned on an Audi just so Garrett could drive to work. I managed to negotiate a deal on a BMW for myself.

After his mortgage company went under, Garrett took a salaried position with the biggest douchebag I'd ever met, a man with a holier-than-thou vibe who only paid him $7,000 per month. I was furious. *I'm barely working, and I can make $5,000, I thought. You don't believe in yourself enough to make at least ten?*

"I'm so appreciative that he's giving me this chance," Garrett said when I voiced these thoughts.

"He's taking advantage of you," I replied.

While working this salaried position, Garrett created a business coaching program called Investors Paradigm, but it didn't take off. He then created Paid to Play, a personal development program that attracted a lot of female clientele and soon became his full-time job. I was just happy that he no longer needed to work for that douche.

Like the restless night after our first big fight in Vegas, I kept debating whether I should stay married. What was the point if Garrett couldn't give me and Bailee security? God knew we weren't enjoying each other's company anymore. Yet divorce seemed scarier than sticking it out.

I was so out of touch with my intuition by then that I couldn't see we were chasing the wrong things, that wealth and prestige only go so far. Blinded by despair, all I could think about was how happy I'd been when Bailee was six months old—and how, according to Mormon standards, I should've already had a second baby. Everyone I knew pumped them out every two to three years.

Though I didn't feel attracted to Garrett at all, I became consumed by the thought that a baby would fix everything. I would be happy, and Garrett would be motivated, and our family would once again be as picture perfect as we seemed right before we hit rock bottom.

Twelve weeks into my pregnancy with my second daughter, I woke up in a puddle of blood. Having had a miscarriage back in Vegas, I thought that I could remain composed, but I was absolutely devastated. Unlike that first time, I had already heard her heartbeat.

The next morning, I visited my doctor and was surprised to find that my baby was still alive and well. The doctor shrugged. "Sometimes that happens," he said. "Just take it easy for the next couple of weeks."

Apart from that initial scare, my pregnancy with Ruby was

uneventful. I was excited to welcome a new member of my family—even if Garrett and I were in survival mode.

Frankly, I didn't know if our marriage would survive past Ruby's birth. Finding out my husband was having an emotional affair after we'd *just* lost our home and cars, while I was *eight months pregnant*—it was too much. I was angry and devastated. I'd never imagined any of this for myself. How much lower could we go? I wanted to mend our broken relationship, but Garrett had already lost my trust. It wouldn't take much to shatter us completely.

I was so consumed by these thoughts that the rest of my second pregnancy was a blur. All too soon, I found myself going into labor at 11:00 p.m. and watching my husband chug a Red Bull so he could stay awake with me. All too soon, we were dropping Bailee off at my parents' house, checking in to the hospital, and getting me prepped for the epidural as normal. Then, just as the needle was being inserted, I heard a loud *thud*.

My head snapped toward Garrett, who was suddenly out cold on the floor. *What the hell?* I wondered as nurses hurried over and put him on a stretcher beside my hospital bed. I was in the middle of getting an epidural, and yet several people were now surrounding my husband.

I didn't have the chance to worry, though, because Garrett quickly came to. "What happened?" he asked.

"You fainted," a nurse replied.

In retrospect, he should've planned to take naps while I was in labor rather than downing an energy drink on an empty stomach. Perhaps he was nervous as we left for the hospital, but I had little sympathy. By then, I was drowning in resentment about our financial state and his emotional affair. We didn't even have insurance and were paying for this delivery in installments.

So when a nurse said that she wanted Garrett to get checked out, I looked at him and said, "You're fucking fine."

He nodded. "Yeah, I'm good."

Funnily enough, we have a picture of us holding hands while he was lying on a stretcher next to me. It was a precarious situation in an already precarious time of our lives, but we were grasping each other through it.

If only that were the worst part of this delivery experience. Just like when I delivered Bailee, the epidural made me vomit, and I didn't know the nurses could give me nausea medicine because no one had ever offered it to me. Somehow the combination of getting sick and feeling numb in my extremities induced a panic attack. Feeling like I couldn't breathe, I started hyperventilating. Everyone told me that I needed to calm down because my baby's heart rate was going up, but I just couldn't get enough air.

The nurses put an oxygen mask on me, but I had to take it off practically every hour of that ten-hour labor so that I could puke. Not only that, but when the doctor popped my water, he saw that my baby had had a fecal accident because of her elevated heart rate. A nurse explained to me that fecal accidents are extremely dangerous; if my baby inhaled during delivery, she'd have to be rushed to the NICU.

So, as I began to push, everyone prepared for emergency procedures. Meanwhile, because Garrett had fainted, he was told he couldn't watch the umbilical cord being cut. He was sent to a corner, like he was in time-out.

The moment Ruby was born, the nurses whisked her away. That was normal in 2011—babies weren't handed to their mothers until they were cleaned, checked, and swaddled—but I was freaking out because she hadn't yet cried. Everyone was moving so fast that I was convinced something was wrong.

Then my darling Ruby let out her first cry, and the whole room let out a sigh of relief. *Thank God,* I thought as a nurse finally gave her to me.

Ruby had thrush, so the first few weeks with her were hard. Nearly any time she was awake, she was crying. But around the time she was feeling better, I was able to start exercising again. I began to train for a marathon, even though, as a postpartum mom, I could barely run a mile.

What I liked most about training for an endurance sport was that it was an almost spiritual experience. I'd begin my runs feeling like I needed to escape from the chaos of my life, to distract myself from my ongoing marital and financial problems, but I'd end them feeling a sense of peace and clarity. Sometimes I could practically hear people cheering me onward; other times I seemed to be downloading ideas and directions directly from God.

Garrett was also training then, for both a triathlon and an ultramarathon. We both thrived on the runner's high, but it almost seemed like we were running away from each other and toward who we were as individuals. For the sake of our preschooler and infant, I could only hope that our paths would eventually intersect again.

Sometime after Ruby was born, I found myself betrayed not only by my husband but also by my community. I was flying with my older sister when she asked if I'd seen the comment a mutual friend had left on Garrett's Facebook post.

It's funny, when you're successful, people will applaud you for taking a strong stance on a topic; when you're struggling, they will attack you for doing the exact same thing. I no longer remember what Garrett's post was about, but I remember that this "friend" just went off on him. As soon as we weren't meeting her standards, she felt comfortable degrading his actions, opinions, even his appearance.

Now, I admit that I felt disgusted by Garrett at that time. After losing his mortgage business, Garrett lost his sense of self entirely. He went from owning crowds on large stages to giving away all his tailored suits and hanging out with home healers. He wore mala beads and walked around barefoot. He wasn't doing any kind of psychedelics—we were still strictly following Mormon practices—but he was going to meditation retreats and questioning everything. He was someone I didn't recognize.

But even if you don't like your husband, it's not okay for others to talk shit about him. If you're going through a hard time, it's not okay for others to cast judgments or fake sympathy.

When the whispers start, it's normal to shut your mouth and put your head down. I knew, and still know, so many people who let others' opinions hold them back. And I get it. It's difficult to continue on the path you're called down when everyone is telling you to take another one.

These days, when Garrett and I coach people who are worried about what their family and friends think, we ask, "Do those people pay your bills? Then you can tell them to fuck off." Often these people are afraid to hurt their loved ones, so we continue, "Would it hurt your grandma's feelings if you prospered? Wouldn't your best friend want you to succeed?"

In 2011, I hadn't yet developed that mindset, but I was getting there. That Facebook comment—and the gossip I'd heard around town—was so hurtful that I realized many in my community weren't true friends. I couldn't live my life based on their opinions.

On the plane, I told my sister, "I'm done with her."

Not long after that conversation, I saw Garrett also grapple with the decision not to let others' opinions control his life. We were at his parents' house, and his father, who is a bishop at their local church, was sharing scripture from the Book of Mormon.

"I don't agree," Garrett said. He'd been studying Buddhism and other religions, and for the first time, he was wondering why we kept following the rules of a faith we'd always felt ambivalent about—which was surprising to me because he was the one who had insisted we stop drinking and start going to church when we got married.

My father-in-law was so mad that he started shaking. "How can you disagree?" he demanded, moving toward Garrett like he was about to throw a punch. "How dare you?"

Garrett's brother and mom had to intervene before things escalated further, and for a while, our relationship with all of them was strained. Mormons believe that if someone leaves the church, they won't go to Heaven with the rest of their family. So Garrett questioning the faith was as good as him saying that he didn't want to spend eternity together. To his dad, it was like his first son was abandoning them—and setting a bad example to boot.

That's why so many from my community are Jack Mormons, people who go out for drinks on Saturdays and then take the sacrament the next day, who hide their skepticism so they don't make others uncomfortable. But if you're constantly worrying about others, you aren't free to create the life you're meant to.

While Garrett and I weren't aligned much in Utah, we were both learning that we didn't want to be held hostage in our own lives. Our families would keep loving us, and they would eventually forgive us. Anyone else could choose whether they wanted to remain in our circle.

In an attempt to reconnect with Garrett, I decided to try the meditation retreats he was so fond of. I'd previously declined his invitations because I thought, *What's the point? You're still not paying the bills. You're not becoming a better man.* But unlike me, he was at least trying to work on himself. Who knew? Maybe I'd get something out of the experience.

Yet a couple of retreats later, I felt more irritated than ever. *Dude, is this it?* I wondered after spending four hours lying on the floor in a dark room lit by candles. By then, I'd tuned out the shamans chanting around us. *What the hell?*

I genuinely tried, but I couldn't connect with the people at these retreats. I couldn't make myself care about the trust falls and tightrope exercises. The only good thing I can say is that the retreats gave me the space to listen to my intuition: *If Garrett is discovering himself right now, maybe he's not supposed to be the provider. Maybe I am.*

It was far from the perfect time to act on this epiphany. My hormones were still out of whack from having Ruby, and our financial picture wasn't looking much better, but I refused to go any lower. The question was no longer, *What do I have to lose?* but instead, *How do I change my story?*

I still thought of myself as "just" a hairstylist—not an artist, not an entrepreneur—but I began to wonder how I might expand. I started bouncing ideas off of Garrett, who loves building businesses, and he was extremely supportive. He suggested that I market myself as a brand, something that was virtually unheard of fifteen years ago.

Back then, there were popular hairstylists like Guy Tang on YouTube, but no one claimed to be an educator or had products they were trying to promote. Who did I think I was? My imposter syndrome could've been debilitating, but I didn't have a choice about continuing or not. We were barely keeping the lights on at home—I couldn't wait to build a following before promoting my hair extensions.

Besides, I'd always been an educator. Ever since I'd created my extensions technique, people had been asking me to explain it to them, and I did—for free. I knew there was demand for my expertise, so I just needed to find a way to package and sell it.

To start, I created a personal blog and YouTube channel promoting my new brand, Natural Beaded Rows (NBR). I won't lie: it was disheartening at first. I realized that while I had nearly ten years of professional styling experience, I was a novice when it came to content creation. I spent several late nights learning to use editing software only to get two hundred views on my first video.

But then I realized that was good. Any first attempt will suck, so it's better if fewer people see it. As long as I kept posting, I'd get more comfortable on camera and better at editing, and soon enough I would have more eyes on my content—and therefore more potential customers.

To my surprise, I got an early boost on YouTube. I'd asked a client whether I could film myself doing her hair in exchange for a good price, and she agreed and even let me film a testimonial. Then she was chosen to be on *The Bachelor*. By the time I edited and posted the video, her name was recognizable enough that my channel blew up.

It was the first indication I had that I could be successful as a hairstylist—that maybe God had put me on the right path.

In the midst of being a mom and an entrepreneur, I found myself rehabilitating Lizzy, our teacup-sized wiener dog. She had a habit of jumping off couches, and one morning, I noticed that one of her back legs was dragging. I immediately took her to the vet, and they said she'd ruptured a disc. We had two options: put her down or pay $7,000 for surgery.

I didn't care that we had no money and that the surgery would just add to our debt. To me, putting Lizzy down wasn't an option. She was my first baby, and she wasn't that old.

Unfortunately, the surgery didn't go as well as the doctor expected. Afterward, Lizzy was in pain, partially paralyzed, and had an estimated 80 percent chance of recovery. I was in shock, but something shifted within me. I wasn't about to give up on her, not after surviving so much other shit the past couple of years.

Lizzy was so tiny that she needed a custom doggy wheelchair, so the doctor helped me take her measurements and send them off. I then watched a ton of videos on taking care of handicapped dogs, including doing physical therapy exercises in the bath. I had a toddler and a baby and was soon sick to death of changing human and canine diapers, but I kept at it.

Just as I was becoming frustrated with the whole ordeal, I had a dream that Lizzy was walking again. When I woke up, I told Garrett, "Lizzy is going to be fine. I saw her. She's going to learn how to walk again."

He was understandably skeptical, but I kid you not, three days later, I saw my determined weenie trying to use her back legs. Her upper body had gotten so strong that she could just let her hindquarters follow in the wheelchair, but I could tell that the wheelchair was annoying her. I took it off, and she started running.

It was such a beautiful, miraculous moment...and then Lizzy started peeing everywhere. Since being partially paralyzed, she hadn't been able to control her bladder, but I was still ecstatic. One thing in our life was almost back to normal, and soon, I hoped, other things would be as well.

What's the sunniest state in the US? I Googled one afternoon when my seasonal depression was particularly bad.

After years of long winters and nasty gossip, I no longer felt that Utah had anything to offer me or my family. I could see, so clearly, Garrett, the girls, and I chilling in a house near a beach in California. But the Golden State was too expensive, even after creating our brands, and I refused to get a two-bedroom apartment or condo with two kids and two dogs.

Arizona, said the search results.

So Garrett and I flew down to Scottsdale, looked at the surrounding areas, and found a house with a pool that was in our budget. But there were a few problems: the rental owner didn't allow pets, the house was half the size of our current rental, and we couldn't afford the move.

"Listen," Garrett said, "I think we should give Lizzy away. We won't tell him about Cloey, but with everything going on, we can't have a dog that pisses everywhere."

I agreed. I was heartbroken—but also exhausted from cleaning up after her. I didn't think I could handle taking care of two girls, one potty-trained dog, and one dog in diapers while settling into a new home and expanding my business.

That's how, a month later, we found ourselves hosting an estate sale, selling couches, clothes, anything we didn't absolutely need out of our home. Garrett even sold the top-of-the-line bike he'd used in an Ironman triathlon in Hawaii, but I was still so resentful that I didn't feel bad for him. I was too busy wallowing at the checkout table, next to a sign that read, "Ask me about my dog."

Toward the end of the afternoon, an older lady did ask about Lizzy. She wanted to know why we were rehoming her and nodded sympathetically when I explained our situation. Her words were so kind, especially compared to the pitying whispers I'd heard all day, but I began to cry when I handed my sweet wiener dog over.

"Don't worry; I'll take care of her," the woman said.

To this day, I don't know who she was, but I believe her. Before she left, a man randomly started being a dick to me. I don't even remember why, probably because I wouldn't negotiate on the price of some item. But that woman came to my defense, like Lizzy connected us.

As hard as it was getting rid of all that furniture and the dog who'd been my companion since the beginning of our marriage, it also, weirdly, felt nice. I realized that I didn't want to hold on to stuff that reminded me of this chapter, of us losing everything. Garrett and I had committed to making Arizona a fresh start, and now it really would be.

Chapter 5

REKINDLING THE SPARK

THE NIGHT BEFORE OUR MOVE TO GILBERT, ARIZONA, Garrett and I took our girls trick-or-treating. Garrett was in a boot because he'd torn his Achilles tendon while doing box jumps during a CrossFit session, but both of us wanted to enjoy our last Halloween in Utah.

That night, as we watched Bailee and Ruby go door-to-door, I felt connected to my husband for the first time since learning about his affair. He was hobbling, but he was with us anyway. We were still living at rock bottom, but we were excited to rebuild together. Then we returned to my parents' house, and Garrett said he was going to fix something in our moving pod.

"Are you sure?" I asked. "You really shouldn't be moving stuff around with your leg torn up like that."

"I'll be fine."

Whatever, I thought, but I shouldn't have ignored my intuition, as usual. Just a few minutes later, while my parents, my kids, and I were eating chicken noodle soup, we heard a loud crash—then a deathly scream.

I rushed outside to find Garrett lying on the ground, crying. It was a shocking sight. My husband is a giant, tough man—yet suddenly he had crumpled. He told me that he'd slipped on the ramp, and we both instantly knew that he'd torn his tendon a second time.

Despite being in excruciating pain, Garrett insisted on waking up early the next morning and driving our family to Arizona as planned. So we made the fourteen-hour journey over two days, and then my husband hopped on the next flight to Utah and took the earliest appointment with his regular doctor. Unsurprisingly, when he called me the following day, it was to deliver bad news.

"Hey babe, I have to go in for surgery tomorrow. The doctor says my Achilles tendon looks like hamburger meat." Garrett paused. "He says he needs to see me every week for the next three weeks, so I'll have to stay with my parents. We don't have the money for me to fly back and forth."

Oh my god, I thought. *Of course. Why not?*

Often, it's when you let go of your past and get glimpses of your future that God tests you. Many people, especially women, take these tests as a sign that they're not supposed to pursue that future. *It's not meant to be*, they think. But this tendency is the result of fear. It's an excuse to stay where you are since what you know seems safer.

I'll admit that there was a moment I questioned our decision to leave home, but even if we wanted to move back, we couldn't afford to. We just had to figure it out. So Garrett went to his dad, whom he'd severely offended, and asked to stay in their basement as he recovered from surgery. Meanwhile, I would spend the next few weeks getting our utilities set up, unpacking our moving boxes, looking at preschool options for Bailee, and trying to find a salon I could work at.

Because Garrett was gone, my mom came down for a week to help me settle in. At the same time, my mother-in-law found the church closest to us and called its bishop. The next thing I knew, people were unloading our moving pod and bringing us home-cooked dinners.

One thing I will say about Mormons: they're all about service. Since short-selling our first home in Sandy, Garrett and I had only attended church sporadically, and these acts of service reminded me just how generous that community can be—even if I didn't fully agree with their beliefs.

Still, I was extremely overwhelmed and anxious. Single parenting for three weeks really put into perspective how much I depended on Garrett, how many things I expected him to do because he was the husband.

Not only that, but I was also supporting my husband emotionally. Garrett has always been active, and it killed him to have to rest and recover. For the first time, I had to take care of him. I had to help him out of a dark place.

Suddenly, I was our family's caregiver *and* provider, but I was surprised to find that I bore both roles well. As hard as those early months in Gilbert were, I felt fulfilled. I was excited to rekindle the spark in my work and relationship while living there.

The problem with finding a salon in Gilbert was that it was a farm town. Back in 2011, you'd pass nothing but silos on your way in, and the stench of cow patties was so pervasive, you had to roll up your windows. Not only that, but all the hairstylists in town charged a fraction of what I did, basing their prices (like many business owners do) on the local going rate. Meanwhile, I wanted to position myself as an elite artist and was too broke to lower my rates (not that I wanted to).

I ended up landing a job at a fancy salon in Scottsdale, but the day before I was supposed to start, I felt in my gut that I shouldn't take it. Yes, on paper, the job looked like the logical next step in my career, but my intuition was telling me I needed to be closer to home. On a good day, it was a forty-five-minute drive to the salon, and I didn't have childcare at the time. In addition, I'd be working on commission instead of renting a booth, since I didn't yet have clientele in the area, and the girl I interviewed with hadn't even been doing hair for as long as I had.

That's all normal in the hair industry, but I had a bit of an ego about it. After spending months creating a brand and positioning myself as an educator, I wondered, *Why should I have to share my profits, especially with someone who doesn't have the skills I have? Why can't I be my own boss?* It was the first time I questioned my industry's norms.

So, with no plan, I called the girl and said, "Hey, I don't want the job."

She was kind of offended, but I didn't care. God was nudging me somewhere else.

That same day, I took my girls to a park and struck up a conversation with another mom. I'm never social, but I started telling her about turning down the job in Scottsdale, and she said, "My friend has a salon/spa studio nearby."

"What's that?" I asked.

She explained how the studio was a building with a bunch of rooms ("booths") that you could rent for your business. The booths were small, but you could work in your own space instead of next to several other stylists. Plus, the studio was walking distance from my new home.

It sounded perfect, so I got the owner's number from the lady in the park. As soon as I left, I called her up and was told I could rent a booth for $300 per month.

"Fair enough," I said. I didn't tell her I could make more than that by doing one client's hair extensions.

If I could get a client, anyway. The women in Gilbert weren't my ideal clientele; as mentioned, they expected much lower prices than I typically charged. Some even had the nerve to ask to trade services. But the only trade I was willing to make was for photos of my work, which I could use to market myself to women who *would* pay up for high-end extensions.

When I first saw my new booth, the idea of positioning myself as an elite stylist in a small town seemed even more far-fetched. The tiny booth's best feature was a Costco painting on the wall! It was then that I realized that sometimes God calls you to humble yourself just when you think you've made it. I could've taken the more prestigious job in Scottsdale, but perhaps I was being humbled so that I could help more people right where I was.

In the beginning, I would fly to Utah every six weeks to do extensions at an upscale salon with tall windows. For three days at a time, I would take photos and videos of my work in a beautiful space, and then I would return to my modest home and use that content to market my services in Gilbert. It took about eight months, but I eventually gained enough momentum that I no longer needed to take clients in Salt Lake City.

Part of gaining that initial momentum was that I also committed to putting out weekly content on my blog and YouTube channel. A couple of days each week, for the two hours Ruby was napping and Bailee was in preschool, I would work on making photo collages or recording and editing tutorial videos. And it's funny because those early videos were like a live stream: my bed was unmade half the time, and sometimes my baby would wake up and start throwing shit in the background. Back then, creators tried to look as professional as possible, so I got tons of mean comments, but I knew that I had to keep at it. I needed money.

"Hi, I'm Danielle, the creator of Natural Beaded Rows," I'd begin, acting more confident than I felt.

To my surprise, many people gravitated toward my content because it was authentic rather than scripted because I let myself be vulnerable when I shared my story. It was scary putting myself out there, but it taught me that your trade is just a tool you use to connect with people.

That's something I teach to this day. It doesn't matter if you're a chiropractor or construction worker or film director; we're all called to connect. People struggle to do this when they feel unqualified, but we all have a story, and those stories can impact others regardless of our current skill levels. The experiences we create matter more than our location, image, or any of the other things we're taught to prioritize.

So I taught myself personal branding through trial and error, and my efforts paid off. Before long, a woman emailed asking if I had people travel to get extensions done, and I requested photos of her hair and scheduled a phone consultation. For thirty minutes, I listened to her talk about what types of extensions she'd tried, then told her that I thought my technique would work for her. I was doing sales calls before I even knew that was a thing. The reality is that sales is about solving a problem; I was simply listening to women and helping them feel beautiful with the only tool I had: hair.

"I'm not the type of person who would take your money if I didn't think I could do it," I promised. "I've been doing this for ten years now. You're in good hands."

That honesty—combined with my willingness to listen to her struggles—sealed the deal. She flew to Phoenix, drove past the silos and cow patties to Gilbert, sat in my booth with the Costco painting, and connected with me in person. And she ended up loving the extensions and our conversation so much that she started flying in every six weeks to get her hair done.

After that success, I began advertising my services for weddings, trips, you name it. People watched my videos because I was relatable, and they booked my services because I always included a call to action (though I didn't know that term back then). I was learning the power of certainty, of believing in your product. I might've lived in a small town and had a low cost of goods, but I could charge my ideal clients a premium because of my positioning online and the quality experience I delivered in person.

After losing everything, we didn't travel. We were no longer even able to visit my stepson, Parker. So I was thrilled when my parents invited Garrett and me to their time-share in Hawaii. All we had to do was pay for our flights and find a babysitter for the girls.

"We don't have enough money," my husband said when I brought it up.

Now, I'm the kind of person who doesn't easily accept no for an answer. I always look for ways to entertain a possibility. So I started checking flights daily and noticed the prices kept going up. I realized the continual price hike was artificial, began clearing my browser history any time I checked, and eventually bought tickets when they dropped low. It was a little thing, but it underscored a lesson I'd been learning in Arizona: innovation can take you further than any established path.

That lesson was underscored again in Hawaii after a conversation with my mom. When she initially told me how my older sister was charging $1,200 for extensions, I was pissed. *How dare she?* I had a pretty website, a growing social presence, and a large book of clients, yet I was only charging $500.

That night, I tossed and turned in bed until a wave of calm came over me. *Why am I so mad at her?* I wondered, empathy slowly replacing envy. *She didn't have a choice.*

My sister and I had actually been connecting a lot recently because we were both going through huge transitions. I didn't know if I would stay married, and she was newly divorced. My family moved to Arizona, and hers moved to Oklahoma. But prior to her divorce, my sister's ex had racked up a couple hundred thousand dollars in credit card debt in her name. Of course she didn't have a choice about how much she charged; she had no credit and had to put food on the table for her kids.

Inspired by my sister's example, I asked myself, *If she can charge $1,200, in Tulsa of all places, why can't I? I already have people willing to fly to see me. And I have to get childcare anytime I fly to clients in Utah.*

It's interesting because, these days, I'm skeptical when I see people charging too little for their services. I wonder what the catch is—or assume it's a scam. Yet I didn't realize back then that I was probably doing myself a disservice by charging less. All I knew was that people in my town liked to complain about my "expensive" extensions at $500.

Oh well. As soon as I returned home, I called my clients and said that I was doubling my price. With childcare, I was only able to take clients three days, so I couldn't fit everybody in.

Almost all of them wanted to book. I was shocked. I'd doubled my price, and everyone still wanted to have me do their extensions.

Within a year of moving, I doubled my income for the same amount of work, had a steady stream of clients flying in, and was wondering how I might expand my business further. That's when I remembered how, shortly before leaving Utah, I'd made $8,000 teaching a class on my hair extensions technique. I then remembered how, when I advertised the same class in Arizona, not one person had signed up.

I was embarrassed at the time. It was clear that the class in Salt Lake was only a success because I had a warm audience there; people already knew me as the extensions girl. So I'd have to try harder here.

Garrett had the idea for me to create a virtual course. Instead of receiving DVDs in the mail, the industry norm at the time, hairstylists could purchase direct access to my online training videos. To create extra income without in-person fulfillment, I just had to figure out how to film, edit, and host content. Easy enough, right?

Using a Sony camera we already had, my husband filmed me doing hair extensions for my clients, and I stayed up late many nights editing the videos. But just like when I started my YouTube channel, I felt so stupid, so unqualified. Who did I think I was, making educational content? Who would ever buy this course? Everyone would know I was an imposter.

One midnight, the darkness of my room broken only by my computer screen, I began to tear up. The video I was editing seemed completely unprofessional, even to a rookie content creator, and I was exhausted. Why was I working so hard on a video that didn't match the quality of my work—that might, in fact, undermine how good I was at hair extensions?

Sobbing now, I threw off my headphones and fell to the floor. *I can't put this out. It doesn't represent me.*

In that moment, I was ready to quit, possibly for the night, possibly forever. Then a feeling of calm came over me, and I heard a voice say, *You have no idea who you'll impact.*

I can't overemphasize how pivotal hearing that message was for me. Though the time between me breaking down and getting up to finish the edit was brief, it changed everything. I knew, to my core, that the late nights and heartache would be worthwhile.

The next day, I published my $500 course on the website I'd built with the help of a couple of girls Garrett was coaching. It was ready, even if it was far from perfect.

In the beginning, I only sold the course about once per week, but I was happy because that was still an extra two grand per month. I knew that I could always update the course to better represent my skills. What I didn't know was that it would remain a source of residual income for years to come.

At the same time that I was building a following online and selling my course, I decided to advertise a shadowing program on my website. If anyone in the Scottsdale area wanted to learn from me in person, all they had to do was reach out. And they did. A couple of girls paid me to come to the studio, watch me do coloring and extensions, assist as needed, and practice on a doll head at the end of the day.

By the time Garrett and I decided to leave Gilbert, I had at least two girls shadowing me every week. It was great. They were learning, and I was making a little extra money while receiving assistance.

Little did I know that there would soon be more demand for my education than I had time for, when you're an entrepreneur, buying back that time is a key part of avoiding burnout.

As part of our commitment to a fresh start in Arizona, Garrett and I made a conscious decision to go on weekly date nights. It wasn't a common practice among married couples in our community; couples didn't see the point of spending money on a date when they were together every day. But after everything we'd been through, my husband and I wanted to reignite the spark between us—or at least try to understand each other.

Sometimes we'd eat dinner in a Taco Bell parking lot, spending more on our babysitter than on the actual date. Other times we'd go to a sushi bar twenty minutes away and get cocktails, feeling more rebellious than we had since college. (At this point, we were one foot in, one foot out the door of the Mormon church.) Either way, we'd pick a topic and spend the evening talking about it, whether that was recent wins for our businesses, tricky interpersonal situations, or just something we'd recently enjoyed.

I think that oftentimes in marriage, people assume they know everything about their spouse and stop checking in with them. They no longer take an interest in mundane conversations like "How was work? What'd you have for lunch?" And they avoid tough conversations that might lead to an argument.

But when our marriage was falling apart, I remember feeling too numb to argue, too worried about losing my security if the argument spiraled out of control. In starting to date again, I realized that it's actually scarier to never argue. If you're not arguing, you're not really in the fight for your marriage. If you're not fighting for your marriage, that's a sign you're not willing to grow.

I didn't want to be someone who got pissed for stupid reasons like my husband turning the doorknob the wrong way. I didn't want to be someone who resented my husband for twenty years, then divorced him and took half his money. To be honest, it might've been easier for me if we got divorced at that time; I was already making enough money that I could get by, and I would have more time to build my business if we split custody of the girls. So I chose to put in the work, not because I had to but because I wanted to fight for my relationship.

Fortunately, date nights gave Garrett and me space to argue more effectively. We knew that we could get our feelings out without the argument escalating too much, because we were in public. And learning to speak candidly to each other led to us communicating better. In fact, these dates became increasingly light and fun, something we looked forward to instead of dreading.

During one of these dates, Garrett told me about his new business idea. For the past couple of years, he'd coached both men and women on sales and marketing, but he didn't feel like it was his calling. He wanted to focus on helping men like him, men who were taught to shove their emotions down and focus on work, feel more fulfilled in every area of their lives.

This self-development program was, of course, born from

Garrett's story. Even though our marriage and businesses were far from perfect, he wanted to share how he lost his cars, home, company, and himself in trying to pursue wealth—how it was only then that he realized how broken our marriage was.

Garrett wanted to share what he'd learned while acknowledging, "I'm still trying to get out of the hole I dug myself over the last seven years." He wanted to give men a safe place to be vulnerable, help them succeed in business, and show them how to be intentional with their relationships, spirituality, and physical and mental health. He wanted to make it clear that every part of our lives is interconnected.

"Yes!" I said, relieved that he was coming out of what I called his hippie-dippie phase. "That sounds like you. I think this program is really going to resonate with people."

Garrett smiled. "I'm going to call it Wake Up Warrior."

Somehow, when we picked our rental, I didn't realize that Gilbert was such a small town. I thought it was part of the nearest city, Scottsdale. But within a month, I couldn't wait for our two-year lease to be up so that we could move to California like I originally wanted. In retrospect, I think getting out of there really incentivized me to scale my business quickly.

By the time our lease was almost up, Garrett and I felt it was time to move on. We took a trip to California and, knowing we couldn't yet afford to live on the water, settled on a rental in Ladera Ranch. It would be a big upgrade—we'd double both our square footage and our rent—but our brands had enough momentum that we felt we could handle it.

Recently, Garrett had hosted his first Wake Up Warrior event at a nearby Hampton, and the energy in the room was palpable. You could tell that all twenty men were hanging on his every word. My husband had always been likable, but now his message truly aligned with who he was.

At the same time, I finally felt like more than just a hairstylist. I was an artist and entrepreneur, and between my online course, YouTube tutorials, and shadowing program, I was also living out my calling: to serve other artists through education.

Though our time in Arizona was short, Garrett and I dismantled many of our limiting beliefs. We found clarity in our purposes. And we started movements that would later shake up our respective industries. We didn't yet realize how far-reaching our impact would be, but we couldn't wait to discover how we could better serve others in California.

Chapter 6

PURSUING PURPOSE

BEFORE WE MOVED TO LADERA RANCH, I SHARED ONLINE that I would soon be taking clients in California, so I was booked by the time we arrived. For a couple of days, I was scrambling, posting on Facebook and talking to neighbors in the hopes of finding a place where I could temporarily take clients.

I ended up renting a chair at a salon in Laguna Beach for a week, but I knew immediately that I wouldn't stay there. The salon was in the middle of town, so the traffic getting there was terrible. And it was a tiny salon, so there was no parking and hardly any space to work.

One day when I was driving home from work, I passed a big, beautiful salon right off the Pacific Coast Highway. Envisioning myself taking clients and enjoying the ocean view from my chair, I decided to stop by and meet the owner. Inside, I complimented his salon, told him about my hair extensions technique, and showed him my social media. I exuded so much confidence that I could tell he was impressed, and he hired me on the spot.

The industry norm for new employees is to sit around and

wait for walk-in appointments, but I wasn't worried about getting regular clients. Because of my online content, my personal brand was gaining momentum. I was confident that I could make money renting a booth right out of the gate, and I was right. Within six months, I had a full book of business again; within a year, I was slammed.

I thought I'd made it. I was now a successful stylist working at a stunning salon in a desirable part of town. The previous year, I'd worked under a Costco painting in a tiny booth in a farm town.

Yet when I started getting too busy to only work half the week, it all started to become too much. Garrett and I hired a nanny for our baby, Ruby, and we found a private school with extended daycare for Bailee, but the school was thirty minutes away from my salon. So, on the days I picked my daughter up at 5:00 p.m., she was the only child still there. I'd find her coloring with the teacher, all her friends already gone.

As if I didn't feel enough mom guilt, in the winter, it was usually dark by the time I picked Bailee up. "Mom, why do you always get me at night?" she asked once.

But I didn't have an assistant, and I didn't feel like I could turn clients away. So I began coming home at increasingly later hours and relying on the nanny to pick Bailee up.

For our first year or so in Ladera Ranch, I would wake up early, pack lunches for my girls, leave Ruby with the nanny, drop Bailee off at school, get to the salon before the owner, and make sure my station was clean and organized. Then I'd spend ten to twelve hours at the salon, working on clients and guiding the stylists who were shadowing me. And then I'd pull into the driveway at 8:00 or 9:00 p.m., cry in my car for a few minutes, wipe away my tears, and go inside to work on content creation and marketing.

Back in Arizona, I was only taking clients three days per week, and Ruby still took naps, so I had plenty of time for personal branding. Now I had until midnight—or whenever I crashed. I was exhausted, but I refused to acknowledge it.

The only day I consistently took off was Sunday, which Garrett and I reserved for family time since we were no longer going to church. (I went once when we first moved but felt uncomfortable, especially because the bishop kept pressuring us to baptize Bailee and Ruby. Garrett took them a few times afterward but only out of shame.) I never felt like I belonged in the Mormon church, and though I moved on emotionally before my husband did, we both decided we wanted a day solely dedicated to connecting with each other and our girls.

But despite connecting with Garrett on dates and mostly being on the same page in our day-to-day, I opened my own bank account. Now that I understood the power in producing, I wanted to track my business expenses and profits; after all, you don't know what to charge if you don't have an accurate idea of what your overhead is. If you don't know what you're making, you can't control it. You'll end up making emotional decisions for your business instead of logical ones.

I also wanted to ensure that money from Natural Beaded Rows didn't get mixed up with money from Wake Up Warrior, given that I was now making ten to twenty grand per month. I even wanted to share my numbers to sell my product, proving to viewers that with the right technique and marketing, you can make a good living. But I wasn't as transparent about the numbers with my husband.

The truth is that while I had plenty of good reasons to keep a business account, I kept the specifics secret because the account was my security blanket. Garrett and I still had plenty of issues, and I wasn't convinced we could work through them. So I began stashing money away in case things went south again—in case our marriage didn't survive whatever came next.

One night on the beach during date night, I could feel Garrett's frustration. He hadn't said it out loud, but it was there—heavy in the silence between us. I didn't know how to approach him without it turning into an argument. And truthfully, I wasn't sure I even wanted to know what was beneath it.

"I don't know if I can..." he said quietly, before I had spoken a single word. He paused, then continued. "I don't know if this marriage is going to work for me if we can't figure this piece out."

Oh. Sex again.

I didn't know why, but even after implementing regular date nights, I didn't desire my husband. I would unintentionally withhold sex for a week or more, and then Garrett would act like a starving man in a desert. Sometimes I felt like he only wanted to be in this relationship so that we could have sex.

But Garrett wasn't threatening divorce; he was admitting to being in a painful place. I decided to hear him out.

My husband told me that I'd be surprised by how many of the guys he coached were in sexless marriages, how they tried to shut off that need as a result. He wasn't willing to do that, so he wanted to figure out what was going on between us.

"Why don't we try therapy?" he asked.

It wasn't the first time Garrett had suggested we seek professional help, but it was the first time I really considered it. I'd always said something along the lines of "You're the crazy one. If you want therapy, you should probably go fix yourself." Like many in 2015, I still considered therapy something shameful, something you only did if you were completely broken.

Yet now my husband, a man who was often explosive, was gently asking me to try therapy with him. Was I really going to keep shoving the sex issue under the rug? Was I going to give up on improving our marriage without exhausting every option? And for what—pride?

Honestly, I was tired of feeling sexually indifferent. Clearly, my needs were not being met either, so maybe it would be a good idea to talk to someone about it.

Now, Garrett and I didn't click with our first few counselors, but once we found the right person, we began going to therapy at least once each week. And I found it surprisingly helpful. Having a counselor was like having a sounding board; she'd tell Garrett how she interpreted what he was saying, and instead of getting defensive like he would with me, he actually processed the feedback. In this space, I felt safe to share my thoughts and feelings—and even to insist that I have a chance to speak.

Through therapy, I started to understand that many women think all they want is security, but they're really looking for connection. Many men think all they want is sex, but they're also looking for connection. If spouses can connect on a deep, emotional level, they can gain a greater awareness of and empathy for each other's needs.

Sadly, a lot of couples ignore early signs of strife in their relationship. They wait until they're at a breaking point, then complain that therapy isn't enough to repair ten years of damage. So take it from a skeptic: seek guidance as soon as you notice negative relationship patterns. You probably wouldn't hesitate to hire a trainer who could help strengthen your body for a competition, so why not see a marriage counselor who can help you communicate your needs?

Over time, I recognized the underlying reasons why I wasn't opening up to Garrett. He recognized the ways that he was contributing to my fears. And these conversations, among others, led to healthier communication.

Finally, we were making progress in our marriage. I hoped that that progress would improve other areas of our lives as well.

One Friday night, after working a twelve-hour salon shift and staring at my screen for another two hours, I fell onto the carpet and began sobbing uncontrollably. *What the hell am I doing? I thought. This is so stupid. What is the point of working this hard?*

At this point, both my and Garrett's brands were making good money. We weren't in survival mode anymore, so I kept questioning why I was tolerating such long days, why I couldn't say no to potential clients.

Garrett's making enough money that he can take care of us. I'm out.

I loved creating enjoyable salon experiences for my clients and seeing them walk out more confident. I loved educating other stylists in person and online, knowing that their impact would be greater than if they kept following the same old rules. Yet the satisfaction of a job well done did not include sacrificing my mental and physical health for work, let alone being (in my mind) a shit mom. I hated the mom guilt every working mother faces—the feeling that you're neglecting your kids.

Why did I feel more alive at work than at home? Why couldn't I fulfill my purpose and enjoy time with my girls guilt-free? Men easily unplug when they leave the house. Why do women give themselves such a hard time?

Maybe I should just quit.

As soon as the thought came, a wave of calm settled over me, and I stopped crying. Then I heard a voice say, *You would be selfish to quit.*

What? I thought. *I'm being a selfish mom.*

The voice didn't say anything more, but the feeling of calm remained. I realized that I didn't have to choose between my kids and my work. I could find a way to feel fulfilled in both areas of my life. So, with renewed purpose, I picked myself up, sat at my computer, finished my project, and went to bed.

The next morning, I told Garrett, "I'm so tired of working Saturdays."

"Then don't work Saturdays," he replied.

"No, no, no. I have people flying to me, and they have jobs, so they have to come on the weekend."

Garrett shrugged. "Who says they have to come on Saturday?"

"I do," I said. In the hair industry, it seemed you could only succeed if you worked weekends.

I went to the salon that day to do a couple of clients' extensions, but I kept thinking about our conversation. I realized that I could continue overworking myself, or I could establish some boundaries.

When I returned home, I looked at my schedule and saw that I had clients flying in for the next six Saturdays. I then looked at my services. Coloring was only 30 percent of my business, so if I stopped offering coloring and doubled the price of my extensions, I could work half the time and make the same amount of money. I would no longer have to work weekends.

This is another example of how much expectations shape our perspective. In truth, I never had to work weekends. It was just an industry practice to accommodate clients, and I thought that I had to be even more accommodating since I had clients flying in. I'd been taught that the only way to have success was to burn yourself out, but refusing to abide by that rule is what ultimately freed me.

That day, I took a deep breath and started calling my clients, explaining that I would no longer be working Saturdays and that my prices were increasing. I offered to book extensions for the soonest available dates, gave referrals to those looking for coloring, and promised to cover any flight cancellation fees.

A few women complained, but most were understanding. And to my surprise, every single one of them rescheduled, even the lady who was bitchy to me on the phone.

Within three months, I was not only working three days per

week, but I was also making more money. I learned what Garrett teaches men: that you can't afford not to spend time with your family. At the same time, I learned that you can pursue your passions *and* be a mom, that mom guilt is sometimes just an excuse not to make moves in your business. It's an excuse to hold yourself back.

I tell hairstylists this all the time: you don't have to choose. In fact, if you go all in on optimizing your business, you'll have to create more boundaries to avoid burnout. As a result, you'll be able to spend more quality time with your spouse and your kids.

Of course, most of us don't learn a lesson once. We learn it over and over, especially during busy seasons of life.

Even after I stopped taking clients on Saturdays, I sometimes spent the day creating content. If Garrett was also working, I would bring my girls to the salon, give them an iPad or coloring book, and say, "Please be quiet for a few minutes. Mommy's going to film."

I felt bad doing that—most Saturdays, we went to the beach or park or stayed home and made cookies—but I was still trying to put out tutorial videos every week. In these videos, I would share my struggles as a wife, mom, and entrepreneur, and sometimes I ended up crying on camera. Talking about my story was like opening a freshly healed wound, but I knew it was a big reason why my sales funnels were working. I wasn't trying to be perfect; I was admitting, "This shit is hard."

Anyway, one time when I stopped filming a video, Bailee came over and gave me a tight hug. "You're such a good mom," she said. "I love you."

I was in shock. Here I was thinking that my daughters weren't paying attention and that I was a bad mom for working with them around, and my oldest indicated that she saw something totally different. She recognized and respected my efforts.

I realized then that, as moms, we often hold ourselves in a prison of guilt, not understanding that our kids notice us living by example—just as my entrepreneurial parents' hardworking mentality was an example to me growing up. In that moment, I felt my mom guilt melting away.

However, I also knew that life can't always be work, work, work. It can't always be sacrifice. You need to carve out time to be with your loved ones, to connect with them. That's why it pissed me off when Garrett and I were driving down the Pacific Coast Highway and he was telling me I should be grateful for everything he was doing.

I snapped. "Do you even know how much money I made last month?"

"What are you talking about?"

That's when I came clean about how much I was stashing in my business account. I told him I was making upward of thirty grand per month between my events, salon, online course, and YouTube channel. I knew that he didn't think my profits were significant enough to make a difference, so the look of shock on his face was gratifying.

That conversation marked a pivot in our business relationship. We intentionally created separate accounts to track our companies' expenses and profits, but we both contributed to and pulled money out of a shared account for our family's bills. He also began to push Warrior more, realizing that he was playing small if his wife could match his numbers while working less.

Not long after, Garrett created Warrior Week, a twenty-person event that was $15,000 per ticket. It was basically a military-style boot camp where traditionally masculine men could do physical activities like carrying logs and swimming in the ocean, then have the space to share their feelings. It wasn't fluffy like most men's programs in those days; it gave students permission to release their emotions without feeling like they needed to hide or sedate. (Like NBR, it actually inspired many copycats...but I'll get into that later.)

Garrett has always been a workhorse. He has more energy than anyone I've ever met, and I sometimes have to slow him down. But that work ethic is part of what initially attracted me to him, and it's what led to Wake Up Warrior's exponential growth.

If our relationship were a boat, I'd be the rudder and he'd be the engine. He trusts me to point us in the right direction, and I trust him to help us get there.

Despite all our success in the town, I didn't particularly like Ladera Ranch. Its suburban atmosphere was familiar because I grew up in a tight-knit Mormon community, but I didn't want kids knocking on my door every five seconds to ask for a playdate. I didn't want to play tennis or sip wine with snooty moms on Friday nights. I realized that while I put myself out there online and in the salon, I was still an introvert; I liked hanging out with my girls going on dates with Garrett and chatting with clients, but I had no interest in getting to know my neighbors.

Besides, I knew Ladera Ranch was a transition because all the way back when we lived in Utah, I'd had visions of my family chilling by the ocean. Plus, I worked in a salon and Garrett had an office space in Laguna Beach. I knew we'd eventually make our way down there; I just didn't know how or when.

Ever since we'd moved to Ladera, Garrett and I would go down to the public beach and walk along the shore to this magical pier that overlooked a brand-new neighborhood. Most beachfront property in California is super old, so you get a lot of new builds next to homes that should be torn down. But this neighborhood had about fifty multimillion-dollar mansions right on the water.

"We're going to live there one day," I told my husband one evening.

He laughed, but I felt the truth of that statement in my gut. I don't believe in the modern interpretation of the word "manifestation"; I don't believe you can just say something and it will happen. But I do believe in the visions I get, and I'm willing to reverse engineer them and put in the work to make them a reality.

I called up my dad, thinking he might be able to help us get a deal since he's a builder with wide-ranging connections, but he told me the lots alone were worth $10 million. I couldn't believe it. I'd seen us there, but that was too much. Maybe in another ten years?

In the meantime, Garrett and I continued working on expanding Natural Beaded Rows and Wake Up Warrior. Before I knew it, our two-year lease was up and we had decided to extend it by twelve months. As much as I wanted to leave Ladera Ranch, I didn't feel like moving. And this way, we'd have a bit more time to finish paying off our debt.

By the time another year passed, Garrett and I had a clean slate, yet we didn't really consider buying a home. I wanted to see how we liked the next area we chose, and my husband had this story in his mind that we still didn't have enough money or good enough credit.

After looking at rental homes in a few towns within fifty minutes of Laguna Beach, we settled on two options, one in Crystal Cove and one in Dana Point. They were about the same size and, again, double the rent we were currently paying. At the time, the market was extremely competitive, but our applications for both were accepted.

Ultimately, the decision came down to location. Everybody around us said we should choose Crystal Cove because it was right next to Newport, which was the place to be. But Dana Point was across from my dream neighborhood, and something about it just felt right.

Chapter 7

MANIFESTING WITH ACTION

AFTER MOVING TO DANA POINT, I CONTINUED TO ONLY work behind the chair three days per week, but anytime I wasn't hanging out with my family, I was thinking about my business. I had so many people shadowing me that education had become exhausting. I figured there had to be a better way.

Seeing Garrett's success with Warrior, I decided to put on events where hairstylists could learn my hair extensions technique, but I didn't realize how much planning was involved. There was booking the salon in Laguna Beach, mailing out kits, ensuring attendees were watching my pretraining videos, getting notebooks ready, and all the other little details needed to host an event. My husband had a whole team at this point, but I was handling all the nitty-gritty on my own.

Not to mention that teaching, in general, is physically and mentally taxing. Once or twice each month, I was on my feet for two days straight, holding space and maintaining energy for ten to twenty students. Yet as exhausting as these events were, I genuinely cared that my students found success.

My events were a success because I knew that what I had to offer was more than just teaching students how to do hair extensions. I had personally experienced so many different mindset shifts since launching my brand that I knew my students would probably need to learn to let go as well, to choose not to abide by established industry standards. So I spoke about it all—hair, business, and purpose.

In the early days, when I was hosting these events at the salon I worked at, students would often come up to me and compliment the space as if it were mine. I never wanted my own salon—I was always more passionate about education but it got me thinking. Perhaps buying a salon and hiring a team would alleviate some of my stress. At the very least, they could help facilitate my classes.

Unlike I had when I made my other business decisions, I didn't act immediately. Truthfully, I told myself that no one could do work as good as mine and that it would cost me time and money to clean up their mistakes. Besides, I was selectively cheap; I didn't even want to pay an assistant.

There was this guy at the salon, though, who was often sitting around waiting for walk-ins. I wondered why he wasn't on social media trying to get leads, but I also felt bad for him. I started to offer him twenty bucks to blow-dry my clients' hair or to prep my space if I was running behind. And eventually, he simply asked to be my assistant.

"How much do you want?" I asked.

"Fifteen dollars per hour."

"Okay, sure," I replied, thinking that seemed cheap.

Having an assistant was, in some ways, better than I could've imagined. The first day, I finished work two hours sooner than usual and dropped by Garrett's office down the street.

"Wow, you're done early," he said. "And you look alive."

In other ways, having an assistant was a humbling experience. I thought of myself as an excellent educator and stylist, yet this kid kept messing up my clients' hair. I realized that I expected him to jump in and know what to do, but he actually needed formal training and clear communication.

These days, whenever I hear hairstylists complain about bad assistants, I tell them, "An assistant can only be as good as their trainer." Training, delegating, and leading are all skills you have to learn when you start managing a team. And, I would find out, I hadn't fully learned those skills when I bought my own salon in Laguna.

Fast-forward a bit to after I'd bought my own salon and started building out a team, and my hair events were so successful that I couldn't keep up with demand. I turned to Garrett, who now led events with hundreds of men.

"Okay," he began, "what we need to do is plan a larger event at a hotel and advertise it as elite training. I'll get some of my team members to handle the sales funnels and email marketing, and you handle your blog and YouTube channel."

"Great," I said.

"And we're going to charge five thousand dollars per ticket."

I was taken aback. I currently charged $1,000 per ticket, and five grand would make my event the most expensive in the industry by far. "That's a big jump," I managed.

But Garrett was right. Thirty students at $5,000 per ticket made the event profitable; if it were any cheaper, we'd lose money.

So we booked a five-star hotel across the street from my salon, and like before, I shared my story and taught my extensions technique. Garrett taught mindset and marketing, helping my students see how they were creating—and could shatter—limiting beliefs. A couple of my new employees assisted as needed, and together we proved that stylists could be artists *and* entrepreneurs. The students loved it.

What's funny is that at the end of these events, we hosted cocktail parties, and my students would stand in line just to have their picture taken with me. I felt like a celebrity, and I hated it. When I wasn't onstage, being among dozens of people made me uncomfortable.

But I didn't want to seem rude, and I understood that these students weren't just coming to learn extensions; they were coming to create a community. And this community had the potential to change the hair industry.

As if he sensed change coming, Garrett came to me one day and said, "Hey, you need to start a podcast."

"What?" I replied. "Hairstylists don't start podcasts."

He was insistent. "We're going to call it *Big Money Stylist*, and you'll talk about all the shit you see in the hair industry."

"That's the dumbest name I've ever heard," I replied, but I decided to trust that this crazy idea was a good one. Most of his were.

For the first couple of episodes, Garrett, two of the hairstylists from my salon, and I crammed together in a tiny studio with four mics. My husband had more speaking experience than I did, and he had been a guest on a few podcasts, so I let him guide the conversation. He had me share my story—how I went from the brink of divorce to teaching my own extensions technique—and then we touched on pain points and wins that students at my events had experienced.

From there, the conversation flowed naturally, even after Garrett left the podcast to me and my stylists. "Why are we working Saturdays?" we discussed one week. "Why are we working on commission?" we discussed another. Every time, we borrowed lessons learned from my salon or events, and we talked about how stylists could do things differently. We empowered them to think outside the box.

As with any skill, it took a while to get comfortable with podcasting, but I had no idea just how much it would improve my ability to tell a story and convey a message. Soon, I could see the difference when I was speaking on stages and online. Better yet, my stylists were gaining enough confidence that I felt I could mold them into trainers. Then they could help run my events.

Big Money Stylist gained popularity very quickly, and within a few years, 80 percent of my students said they found out about my events and online course through the podcast. It was a great lead magnet. Sure, there were bad reviews from people who called us a cult, but negative feedback always trails success. If some people don't get what you're doing, that's a sign you're following your uniquely designed path.

While we were living in the Dana Point house, Garrett also suggested that we start a podcast together called *Date Your Wife*. This time, I was not shocked. One date night, as we were laughing about marriage and parenthood, I said, "Can you imagine if people could actually listen to our conversation right now? I bet they'd find value in it."

"Or they'd think we're a shit show," Garrett joked.

I didn't know about podcasts at the time, but as soon as I put the thought out there, I could see it. Us setting up a camera and sharing our stories—good, bad, and ugly. People watching, listening, applying the lessons to their own lives. The vision was so clear that it felt like it'd already happened.

So Garrett asking to start a podcast with me felt serendipitous. We started soon after.

Interestingly, the podcast became another day of therapy for us. We'd pick a topic sex, work-life balance, whatever we were recently discussing or arguing about at home and talk about it.

It was a way for us to have constructive conversations without getting into a full-blown fight.

Yet there were times when we did fight. There were times when I walked out in the middle of recording. And we still published those episodes. Marriage is hard, and we weren't going to be that couple who's always giving advice, because we were going through the same shit as anyone else.

To my surprise, those episodes are what really resonated with listeners. They would write to tell us, "Oh my god, I love that you posted that. That was so real." And I was glad because we were doing what we had set out to do.

Between therapy, my events, and the two podcasts, I was finally finding my voice. I was no longer allowing Garrett or anyone to steamroll me, and I was unabashedly speaking my truth.

Thank God, because I would need my voice in the coming years.

Back when we lived in Arizona, I had a girl who owned a big salon shadow me and come to me for extensions. When we moved to California, she'd travel every six weeks to have me do her hair. Then, all of a sudden, she stopped coming. She launched a hair line and was basically teaching my system of hair extensions with her hair line, and I ended up suing her.

At first, I had so many clients that I didn't really think much about this. Probably she had just found someone closer who could do her hair. But after a while, clients started sending me videos and screenshots from her social media platforms. "Isn't this NBR?" they asked.

It was. She was teaching my method, and now she had more followers than I did. I had no doubt that I'd soon be losing clients to her.

She can't do that, I thought, stung. I'd poured so much time and energy into teaching her and doing her hair that I couldn't believe she'd take credit for my work. How could she think that was okay?

I reached out to a few lawyers, but they all said that there wasn't much I could do, that suing would be a waste of time and money. But I wanted to protect my brand. I needed to safeguard what I'd built over the last several years.

One of Garrett's clients, who happened to be a lawyer, told me that we could go after her for stealing intellectual property. So we did. But because I never had the stylists who shadowed me sign any contracts, the lawsuit was long, and we ended up settling. The agreement we came to was that she could still teach, but she could not teach or demonstrate NBR. She had to acknowledge that I taught her as well as create her own technique by using different beads, different hair, different methods. That way, we had brand separation.

My first lawsuit taught me a few important lessons. First, it's important to have contracts, even if they won't stave off every copycat. Second, at every level you reach, you'll start out a rookie; there will be things you won't know to do until they bite you in the butt, so you have to be willing to make mistakes and learn from them. Third, because anything that shakes up an industry will invite spin-offs, you have to continually innovate.

Since that first lawsuit, I've realized you have to play if you want to be in the business game. Every time a software program becomes popular, someone will duplicate it and add new features. The original developer will then tweak their program further. The more successful business is the one that pushes their products harder and markets them better.

You have to continually ask yourself, *What problem am I solving in my industry? How can I empower people through my products and services? In what ways can I do it differently than my competitors?*

That's ultimately why Natural Beaded Rows has been consistently successful, even when it wasn't the most popular brand in the industry: I wasn't just teaching hair. I was teaching business. I was teaching mindset.

Around the same time that I sued my former client, Garrett sued a former friend, a guy who had recently started a similar men's coaching program. But unlike mine, his lawsuit went on for years, to the point where it became a huge waste of money. Eventually, Garrett flew to meet this guy in person, offering a box of cigars as an olive branch. There, they realized that while their personalities and messaging were alike, they weren't really in competition. Their audiences were completely different.

That's something else I learned the hard way: you're not going to be everyone's cup of tea. Yes, sometimes you need to fight to keep your brand's clients, but sometimes you need to let go of the people who don't resonate with your personality and message. Let them find their people, and your people will find you.

With all the lessons I learned through my lawsuit, I made my events, online course, podcasts, and social media content even better. Before long, I had so many word-of-mouth referrals that I didn't have to run ads. In particular, I was wait-listing so many people for my thirty-person events that I wondered if I should do larger ones.

With Garrett's help, I planned and hosted a high-ticket, three-day event with two hundred students. It went so well that we soon had three hundred students, then four hundred. I began doing these events up to three times per year, and it really put my brand on the map because no individuals in the hair industry were doing events half as large.

In trying to constantly innovate, I started positioning stylists from my salon as experts and giving them space to train students as well. I invited people onto my stages who had millions of followers, even though I had maybe fifty thousand. But what really struck students was an exercise I implemented called "hot seating."

During this exercise, Garrett and I would ask students a series of questions that led to their pain point. "I can't raise my prices." "I'm working with a client that I absolutely hate." We helped them discover what was holding them back from success and challenged them to overcome it.

One time, a girl was giving us a whole list of excuses about why she couldn't fire a client who was draining her emotionally. "I...I tried," she said. "I told her she could have three more appointments with me." But the client kept coming to her even after those three appointments.

"You're going to call her right now and fire her," Garrett said.

"Oh, no. I can't do that," the student replied, but we could tell she desperately wanted to be free.

"Why not?" I asked.

The crowd, which was experiencing this pain with the student, started cheering for her to do it. She looked at us, teary-eyed, and we encouraged her to come onstage. Once she did, she took a deep breath, gathering her courage, and called the client.

It went to voicemail.

"Listen," I told the student, "tonight, I want you to send her a text saying that your time together has come to a close. Tomorrow, we'll bring you back up onstage, and you can share what she said."

"Don't come back if you're not ready to share," Garrett added.

"Okay," she said.

The next day, it was obvious that this student hadn't slept. But when she read the texts out loud, we learned that her client had simply responded, "No problem. I respect your decision. Thank you for letting me know."

The crowd erupted with applause.

I think often we create these crazy stories in our head about what others will think or say when, really, they just want us to be direct. As I would soon learn myself, you have to be honest about what is and isn't serving you. Otherwise, you're just holding yourself back.

Despite focusing on men in his own business, I think Garrett secretly liked the attention he got when coaching women. He wouldn't have been so involved in my events if he didn't. But his marketing and training tactics were more aggressive than I liked. My brand was becoming more his vision than mine. It got to a point where I wanted to keep working with my husband's team but not with him.

Besides, working together so much wasn't healthy for our marriage. Since the money from my events was going into our shared account, it was difficult to track who was making what. I'd feel resentful whenever Garrett would put out ads for Warrior using money I'd made; he'd feel resentful that he was putting in so much work for NBR while also building his company. We both were successful, and that success made it feel like we were in competition.

The roller coaster of managing my team and competing with Garrett and raising my girls became so much that a part of me, once again, wanted my husband to just take over. I wanted to just be a mom for a little bit.

As always, there was drama with my husband's ex that made it difficult for us to see, let alone connect with, his son, Parker. Whenever they visited, my in-laws read scripture to our girls, which irritated me even though I knew they did it out of concern. Cloey, the wiener dog Garrett had given me for my forgotten twenty-first birthday, died tragically. At times, it was hard to believe we were on the right path. It was hard to keep being a mom and an entrepreneur, to not let the world dictate our next steps.

Maybe Garrett was feeling that way, too, because out of the blue one day, he asked, "Do you know who Tony Robbins is?"

"I think so. He's some guru, right?"

"Yeah. His son came to one of my Warrior events, so if you want to go to Date with Destiny, I can probably get us tickets."

I wasn't familiar with the six-day event Date with Destiny, so Garrett showed me Tony Robbins's Netflix series. "Wow, that's totally different," I said. Unlike the meditation retreats Garrett and I had gone on on, I thought that I might actually get something out of the event. I thought that we might set goals together, since we tended to focus on our own things. We might even determine whether we were on the right path or whether we needed to adjust course.

There were several memorable moments from Date with Destiny, but what stuck with me was what they called a "vision quest." Basically, we were told to write down anything we wanted to achieve in the following twelve months. If we wanted to travel, wanted a Ferrari, wanted our marriage to look a certain way—whatever—we were supposed to put it down on paper.

"Dream big," the trainer said.

I tended to play things safe, to tell myself that certain dreams could only be achieved five or ten years down the road. I didn't want to disappoint myself by not meeting a goal. But for the first time at this event, I opened my mind to what was possible in a year. I wrote quite a few things down and felt a weight being lifted from me.

The biggest and most important goal on my list? Buying a home in the Strand, my dream neighborhood.

Garrett didn't think I was serious when I told him, but as soon as we returned home, I found a Realtor. Despite what my husband thought, our credit wasn't trashed anymore. We had a significant amount of money in savings. We could entertain the possibility of buying a house.

That's why, the day Garrett said he wanted to buy a Lamborghini, I lost my shit. If he was going to get a Lamborghini, then I was going to get a house.

By that time, I knew you couldn't just speak what you wanted into existence; you had to work for it. You had to manifest with action. So I called a Realtor and booked an appointment to view a home in the Strand.

The afternoon of the appointment, I wore a cute, conservative outfit...and Garrett arrived late in a tank top and baggy sweatpants. He exuded I-doubt-we're-getting-this-home-and-I'm-just-placating-you energy. I was mortified, but funnily enough, the Realtor loved him. People are drawn to my husband because he's so comfortable in his own skin, so unafraid to be himself.

Despite Garrett's initial apathy, he fell in love with the house and the area. I could practically see the light bulb shine in his mind when he realized living in a place like that might be possible for us. So, over the next couple of months, we toured more houses, went back and forth with the Realtor, and applied for a loan.

We got approved for $2 million, proving that our credit was much better than Garrett had assumed. But the homes we were looking at were $8 million. We briefly considered buying in another neighborhood, but I didn't want to settle. Then we considered renting in the Strand, but our Realtor said none of the homes were available for rent.

At my wit's end, I finally asked, "What about a lease option? Would somebody be willing to do that?"

"You know what?" the Realtor responded. "There's a guy who built a house out here as an investment, and he's just been sitting on it. Let me see if he'd be interested."

Long story short, that owner agreed to do seller financing. We put $2 million down in cash, plus the $2 million the bank had approved, and we had twelve months after we moved in to take over the rest of his $8 million loan. I was so happy, I offered to use my money to pay for all the furniture we needed to fill the six-thousand-square-foot space.

When Garrett bought our family a house after years of renting, I finally felt secure. I felt like everything would be better between us from now on because I had physical proof of his commitment.

"We fucking did it," I said.

Chapter 8

CHOOSING GROWTH WITHIN ABUNDANCE

KNOWING WE WERE MAKING A HUGE LIFESTYLE LEAP motivated Garrett and me to rapidly expand our businesses, and incredibly, we generated enough cash to fully buy our house in the Strand only six months after we moved. I was thrilled. Somehow we'd gone from selling furniture out of a rental in Utah to owning a multimillion-dollar home in California.

If only things had been going so well at my salon. As we were moving and settling into our new home, I learned from one of my employees that my top stylist/trainer had been acting entitled and resentful at work, like she was better than the other stylists and me. Following her example, the rest of the team started behaving disrespectfully, but I thought I could handle that. Then I found out she was building her own salon behind my back—and planning on poaching my whole team and clientele.

In the hair industry—and perhaps in other industries as well— it's not uncommon for entrepreneurs to blur the line between employee and friend. You pour so much time and energy into the people who work for you, hoping they become self-sufficient, that you become invested in their success. The ultimate goal of entrepreneurs, so they say, is to replace yourself.

The problem is that thinking of your employees as friends makes you reluctant to communicate expectations with them; you don't want to jeopardize your perceived friendship. But once they start having success and you start giving them space to do as they please, they start feeling entitled. They forget who put them in that position, and they act like they've been mistreated, believing they can have the same success without you. Then they leave and realize just how much you did to build them up, to maximize their potential.

Now, I have to hold myself accountable: I could have avoided the heartache of losing my team and clientele if I had communicated better. If I hadn't assumed everything was good, I would've noticed sooner that my top trainer was ready to move on. We could have set up an exit plan for her. Not only that, but I could have established when I hired her and the others that I would fight for my clients. I could've put in their contracts that they couldn't set up a new salon within a fifteen-mile radius of mine. That way, I wouldn't lose half my clientele when they left.

But I didn't know all that as a new business owner. At the time, I felt betrayed. My top stylist/trainer was an amazing colorist, but when she started working for me, she was painfully introverted. I was the person who saw her wit, her skill, and pushed her to shine, training her on my technique, inviting her on my podcast, and putting her on my stages. She was the person who I trusted most, who I thought might lead my salon in a few years.

"What do we do?" I asked Garrett. I couldn't imagine firing her or anyone else on my team. I might've only gone into the salon a few days each week, and I might not have done the best job training them I was still new to leading but I truly considered them my friends.

Another important lesson learned: being friendly is not the problem. The problem is refusing to define the relationship as employer/employee. You have to be careful who you bring into your inner circle because you don't want to give the people who work for you too much perceived power. Don't ignore red flags because you want to keep the peace; establish and maintain clear expectations to create a positive work culture. With a reputation for being communicative, you can more easily course correct when something's not right, avoiding a total implosion.

I'm not proud of this, but when it looked like everything I'd built was about to blow up, I chose to let Garrett handle the situation. One afternoon when I was home with my girls, he called my team to a meeting and said that we were planning on firing my top trainer. Everyone else had twenty-four hours to decide if they'd like to stay.

It was an aggressive meeting, one I was selfishly glad I missed. Yet I wondered if I should've gone, shown that I cared. Maybe then most of my team would've stayed instead of choosing to work with the girl who betrayed me.

I felt so bad that I swore to myself I'd never let him fire any of my team members again. I would be responsible for my own business—my people, my mistakes. And I have been. It's hard to see the pain in an employee's eyes when you let them go, but taking responsibility gives you the opportunity to empathize and offer support. I wouldn't trade it now.

But right then, I had to decide how to move forward, and I chose to take the lessons I'd learned from this salon walkout into my next chapter. I'd built my business from the ground up, and I could do it again. This time, better.

Despite the drama with my salon, I was happy in the Strand.

Garrett and I were financially stable, emotionally available, and at long last, sexually connected. In this comfortable place, I started thinking again about having more kids.

I'd gotten pregnant with Ruby because of cultural pressure and the misguided belief that a baby would fix my marriage. After learning about Garrett's affair, I was afraid to have another child, even though I felt like I wasn't done. I didn't want to bring another baby into a home that wasn't sturdy, but that wasn't a problem now. The only potential problem was that I was in my mid-thirties.

Garrett and I started to try, and within a few months, I was expecting. We were ecstatic. But one day, when I was watching a movie at the theater with Bailee and Ruby, I felt a gush of fluids come out. *Oh no*, I thought. I hadn't yet seen a doctor, but I knew from my previous miscarriage what was happening.

"We have to go," I told the girls.

"Mom, are you okay?" Bailee asked as I stood up. "What's wrong?"

I pulled off my sweater and used it to wipe up the pool of blood on my seat, then rushed my daughters out of the theater. When we got to the car, I told them, "Mommy just lost her baby."

"What do you mean?" Bailee asked.

The girls were old enough to know I was pregnant, but they, of course, had never heard of a miscarriage. I explained as best as I could...and held them when they started crying.

When I saw a doctor, I was told that I didn't need a D&C like I'd had with my first miscarriage, but I would be considered high risk if I got pregnant again. I would need to be closely monitored to ensure the baby and I were both safe. But I was more sure than ever that I wanted another child, so I was willing to take the risk.

Little did I know that, in the meantime, I would become more of a mom to my stepson. Parker had gotten a football scholarship, and we'd promised to pay the rest of his college tuition, but early in 2019, his mental health dropped to an all-time low. He asked to live with us and work for his father.

I'll admit that I was hesitant at first. Though we visited Parker a few times each year, we didn't have a strong relationship with him. We didn't know him that well. Because I had two daughters, I was worried about him bringing drugs or girls into the house, but I shouldn't have been concerned. It turned out that he was a gamer who generally kept to himself—to the point where I had to remind him that he was welcome at family dinners and hangouts.

A huge turning point for our family was when Garrett hosted Warrior Woman. This was his first and only women's event, so he invited his mom, sisters, and even his ex-wife since Parker would be helping out. But none of us could've guessed what would happen.

Just as we did at my hair events, Garrett brought students onstage so they could break down limiting beliefs together. Things were going well—the whole audience was hyped up for the next big breakthrough—and then my husband called me, Parker, and his ex onstage. "Listen, we're going to get some shit out," he said.

Garrett's ex had a lot of resentment because of the amount of child support my husband gave her and because of how infrequently we saw Parker. Parker had resentment toward his mom because he was like a father figure to his younger siblings, who were from two other marriages. He also had resentment toward his dad, who he felt had abandoned him his whole life and was now acting like a savior.

As his ex and son screamed and cried and threw him under the bus in front of four hundred women, Garrett stood there. The only things he said were words of encouragement, like "Let it out." He calls this exercise "releasing the rage," and participating in it gave our family the space to share all our feelings.

Once everyone had said their piece, we all began hugging and crying, and I knew our relationships would be healthier moving forward. In particular, Garrett gained an awareness of when he was acting like a boss or a Disneyland dad at home. And I gained more trust from my stepson, who began to confide his frustrations and concerns in me.

Nowadays, when people ask how many kids I have, I say five. In my mind, Parker became my son when he lived with us, and not long after, my family would be completed with two more beautiful girls.

Over the following months, I hired and trained a new team of stylists, and I was committed to managing them better. Even after getting pregnant once more, I came to the salon three to four days per week and made a point of getting to know everyone. I didn't want to lose my whole team again.

I was also in the middle of a couple of new projects. First, I created my own hair line, which I called Isla. I didn't yet know that I was having another girl, but when I found out, I decided to give my baby the same name. It felt meaningful for my third daughter to share a name with a part of the business that was so important to me.

Second, and more of a time commitment for me, I adapted my old online course into a formal academy. It was 2019, and I was looking for ways to streamline my business. For a while now, Garrett and I had been leading a mastermind program where artists could get weekly training calls and quarterly events for $500 per month. I liked offering such direct support, but the events were so expensive to put on that even with two hundred members, we were barely breaking even. That's when I started considering virtual learning, even though it wasn't popular at the time.

Working with my team, I created a curriculum that would effectively mold artists into entrepreneurs, including topics like extensions and coloring, photography, social media marketing, and contract creation. In addition to these online videos, students would get two in-person trainings. Little did I know that the world would soon shut down because of COVID-19, exponentially increasing demand for virtual learning. It was yet another reminder that sometimes God, your intuition—whatever—is setting you up for success when society is telling you a course of action doesn't make sense.

But being pregnant is hard on your body in the best circumstances, let alone when you're on your feet all day doing hair and creating content. In the second trimester, I started to develop what looked like bruises all over my legs. In fact, people began asking, "Is everything okay at home?" so often that I wore long dresses most days. Yet my doctor just said they were varicose veins.

I tend to be a stress ball, so it was nice that my doctor was funny and relaxed—at first. But I became more and more irritated every time I brought up my concerns and he insisted, "No, you're fine. Don't worry about it. Just wear compression tights."

By the time I was seven months pregnant, I couldn't stand for long periods. The back of my knee was so purple and swollen that I limped around the salon. My team noticed, and one of the stylists eventually shooed me away from my client and asked to see my leg.

"That looks really, really bad," she said. "You should call your doctor."

"I did. He said I'm fine."

She rolled her eyes. "You're not fine. I know you're not a dramatic person, but you need to call him and demand they check again. I'll call if you won't."

So I got an appointment and had some scans done, still thinking it wasn't a big deal. Then Dr. Funny Guy said, "The results have come back. I need to talk to you and your husband."

After sitting me and Garrett down, my doctor explained that

I had deep vein thrombosis (DVT), which is essentially a blood clot issue. If the DVT broke off, it could move to my heart and kill me. They were going to put me on blood thinners and monitor me even more closely, but this time, the doctor didn't say everything was fine—because he didn't know.

I already have anxiety, but finding out about the DVT made it even worse. *Why did I choose to get pregnant again? I* wondered. *Maybe the miscarriage was a sign that I'm not supposed to have another baby.*

My doctor told me that I needed to stop going into the salon, that I was officially on maternity leave, but my interest in work had vanished anyway. *What does it even matter? I should be home with my kids. I caused this by working too hard.* There was no proof of that, but I felt like a piece of shit anyway.

I was so stressed during the last month of my pregnancy that I had terrible panic attacks. If I sat too long, I might have clotting; if I stood too long, I might have clotting. I was bored and tired and worried, and my blood pressure kept rising.

When I went in for a checkup at thirty-five weeks, a specialist told me that I was on the verge of preeclampsia and would need to be induced. I was fine with that—I was sick of being pregnant—but I couldn't have painkillers within twenty-four hours of taking blood thinners. They wanted me to go ahead and come into the hospital, but I'd have to wait a bit to have the baby.

Or so we thought. The next morning, my doctor said that my heart rate kept spiking, so they were going to start the induction even though I couldn't have pain meds for another seven hours. I trusted his judgment, but I had never experienced such intense pain. I had the sweetest nurses trying to coach me on breathing through the labor, but the contractions were far more intense than during a natural labor. At one point, when I thought that

I might pass out, I had an out-of-body experience, like I had to spiritually remove myself to get through it.

After I'd suffered for hours and hours, the blood thinners wore off, and I was given the epidural. Thirty minutes later, before I'd gone numb, the doctor said it was time to deliver my baby.

"I can still feel everything," I said.

"Well, the baby's here. We've got to go."

Let me tell you, the ring of fire is real. The whole hospital probably heard me scream.

What's funny is that when they handed my newborn to me, I thought, *Whose baby is this?* If I hadn't just seen her pop out, I would've thought there was a mix-up, given that my older girls have my darker coloring. But my sweet Isla had an inch of platinum blonde hair, taking after my blond-haired, blue-eyed husband. She was so freaking cute.

Fortunately, Isla was also an easy baby. Sure, it was a bit tough having a newborn again after so many years, but she got on a sleep schedule quickly. She hardly cried and never needed or wanted a Binky. Bailee and Ruby were as obsessed with her as I was, and Garrett was more helpful than he had been with the older girls, even getting up early with her so that I could sleep in.

Now that my life wasn't at risk, I went into the salon once in a while to lead my team and do hair, but I hadn't regained my passion for being behind the chair. All I wanted was to hang out with my family. Let my salon manager run everything.

After Isla was born, everyone told me, "Oh, don't stress about losing the weight. You look great." I knew they were trying to be supportive since I was an older mom and had had DVT, but I didn't like looking in the mirror. I didn't feel like myself. I'd lost most of the seventy pounds I gained during the pregnancy, but the remaining fifteen was a lot on my petite frame.

I don't accept this, I thought. *I want to be a powerful mom for my girls.*

Like Garrett, I'd always been active, but there were times when I was overexercising and undereating to look a certain way. As much as I wanted to get my body back, I didn't want to fall into those old patterns.

That's when I started looking into bikini competitions. *How scary is that? I thought. They have to go onstage half naked. I don't know if I could...and who does bikini competitions in their late thirties anyway?*

But I liked the physique, and now that I was spending more time at home than at the salon, I had quite a bit of energy to burn. Plus, I suspected that training for a competition would help me avoid guilt-based exercise, when you work out as punishment for having unhealthy foods. So I made doing a bikini competition my 2020 New Year's resolution, promising myself that I would follow my trainer's and nutritionist's guidance.

As someone who has both an online academy and in-person classes, I often hear stylists complain about losing clients or not having enough leads when I know that they're not taking my advice. People do this all the time; they hire a coach but lie or make excuses in response to constructive feedback. But I wasn't going to pay people just to ignore what they had to say. I was going to trust their expertise and trust the process, allowing them to hold me accountable and course correct as needed.

Prior to training for bikini competitions, I was a cardio bunny, addicted to the endorphins you get when your heart rate is up. Weight lifting didn't give me the same high, and I thought it was the most boring shit ever. So I had to make a mental shift, chasing results instead of the high of the day.

At the same time, I was keeping a food diary, tracking even the dinosaur nuggets and handful of Goldfish that I consumed between running errands. Doing this, I discovered how many empty calories I actually ate, learned about things like macros and body composition, and made changes accordingly. My nutritionist and I even built a weekly cheat meal into my schedules so that I felt like there was a light at the end of the tunnel.

Within six weeks, I'd lost almost all the remaining pregnancy weight. I was tighter and looked better, proving the truth of "consistency is key." Then, a month before my scheduled competition, COVID-19 shut the world down.

Unlike many, our family was fortunate during the pandemic. My academy now had close to four hundred students, and Garrett and I both created and launched successful virtual events. People still wanted their hair done, even if they had to wear masks, so we reopened the salon as soon as we were allowed. We were comfortable financially, and for the first time, we had an excuse not to work so much.

I remember 2020 as a good year for my family. Parker created TikToks with my adorable toddler, Isla. Garrett and I became very close with all our kids, and we had the opportunity to visit Mexico a few times together. I even continued training for my postponed bikini competition, using hand weights in my garage. I was genuinely happy—and so, so grateful.

After months and months of delays, my first bikini competition was finally scheduled for the fall of 2020. It was such a relief because the prep you do for competition—the strict diets, the intense workouts—isn't sustainable. You're not supposed to maintain that lifestyle for more than four months, but I did it for most of the year.

During "peak week," the week before the competition, my trainer cut back my workouts, saying I didn't want any extra inflammation. My nutritionist told me to drink a gallon of water every day until forty-eight hours beforehand, when I would cut my water intake in half so that my veins would stand out. I was given an almost-purple spray tan that I was promised would look great on stage, and since masks were mandatory, I bought a sparkly one to match my bikini.

Trust the process, I reminded myself.

The weekend Garrett, the kids, and I went down to San Diego for my competition, I didn't recognize myself. While I'd always been into fitness, I had never been so shredded. I wore a sexy dress to dinner, flaunting what I'd worked so hard for, and enjoyed (most of) the steak that my trainer insisted I eat, claiming that it would fill in my muscles just in time for the competition.

"Wow," Garrett said that night. "You're radiating."

"Oh, hun, it's just the spray tan," I joked.

He smiled. "It's not just the way you look. You're standing taller. Your energy is completely different."

It was. I felt confident—and proud that I had stuck with my New Year's resolution despite the pandemic. I realized then that it doesn't matter how you place; if you put in the work and step on that stage, you've already won just by being up there. And the same could be said for any big goal.

I ended up doing pretty well, though. Standing on that stage, hearing that I got first in one category and second and third in a couple of others, I only wished my family were in the audience. Because of COVID-19 protocols, they had to watch on a TV screen in the lobby.

I made the decision then to compete once more, under more normal circumstances, but I'd seen enough to know I didn't want to go pro. Depleting yourself of water and carbs is not sustainable; even after a couple of days, you start to feel loopy. Because of that, it's not realistic to maintain a six-pack year-round, yet too many women get discouraged when they start regaining fat. They get into a dark mental place and develop an unhealthy relationship with dieting and exercising.

I didn't want that; I just wanted to prove to myself that I could do the whole thing again. Training for a bikini competition not only taught me so much about strengthening my body and manipulating the way it looks for short periods; it was also the biggest lesson in trust and perseverance I'd ever had.

And I'll tell you what: the giant cheeseburger I ate afterward tasted damn good.

One night, I was sitting in the hot tub with my family, looking across the bay and thinking about my life—how Garrett and I had worked on our marriage, built thriving businesses, paid off our debt, repaired our credit, and bought a home in our dream neighborhood. I would've never thought any of it possible when everything was falling apart.

Then I heard a voice inquire, *If I asked you to go again, would you?*

I didn't hesitate. *Yes.*

Chills went through my body, and I thought, *Oh shit, what did I just sign up for?*

Sometimes, just when you think you've made it, you're called to do more, and it can be scary to accept that call. It's relatively easy to make drastic changes when things are bad, when it feels like you're drowning, when you're trying to climb out of the hole you've dug yourself—after all, what more do you have to lose? But when things are good, you might not want to upset the status quo. What if things get bad again?

On the other hand, what if you get too comfortable and stagnate? We're all meant to keep learning throughout our lives; that's how we create and act on new opportunities. So we must choose growth even within abundance.

I had the feeling that God wasn't asking if I'd go again because what I had and what I'd done already weren't good enough. He was telling me that there was more I was meant to do, more people I could positively impact.

Not long after, I was walking down the beach when I saw a contractor outside a twelve-thousand-square-foot house that was on a corner lot near ours. This house had been built by a guy from Saudi Arabia who threw a couple of extravagant parties but only stayed in it for maybe two weeks total. Wondering what was going on, I approached the contractor.

Apparently, the house was being finished so that the guy could sell it. With the world still frozen and election season drawing to a close, he just wanted to offload the property. So, out of curiosity, I asked if I could see it.

"Well, it's not on the market," the contractor said, "but I'll find out if you can take a look."

For the past couple of years, I'd wondered what it might be like to live in a beautiful, massive home like that. It was a dream, one I thought might only be possible in another ten years. When Garrett and I toured the home, however, I knew it was ours; we just had to figure out how to get in.

After some back and forth, the owner agreed to seller-finance the house for $24 million. That was triple what we'd paid for our current home, but it was an incredible deal considering he built it for $28 million. Garrett and I decided to take the leap of faith, knowing that every time we jumped, we grew both financially and as a family.

If I learned anything while living in our first house in the Strand, it's this: taking risks is less scary the more you do it. You might encounter speed bumps and detours, but that's all part of the journey. You just have to keep driving.

Chapter 9

LETTING GO

THE WEEK BEFORE MY SECOND BIKINI COMPETITION IN April 2021, my period didn't show up. I was normally pretty regular, but I wasn't worried. I figured that my period was late simply because I was so lean from peak week.

A few days after the competition, though, I still hadn't started, and I suddenly had a little bit of a gut. *What the hell is going on?* I wondered. Including my miscarriages, I'd been pregnant five times, so I understood my body during pregnancy. I thought there was no way I was expecting.

Yet when I took a pregnancy test, it was positive. My heart dropped. I then took several more just to be sure.

For a while, I'd thought about having another baby so that Isla would have a playmate, but I didn't really think it was a possibility given how complicated my last pregnancy was. In fact, when we moved to the second Strand house, Garrett and I gave away most of our baby stuff, thinking we were done. Now I had worked hard to get in shape, and I was expecting again? I was in shock—and frustrated.

There's a special place in Heaven for women who love being pregnant. I love little moments like when the baby first starts kicking, and of course I love seeing and raising the baby when they're born, but I don't love pregnancy itself. Even before I was considered high risk, I felt like my body wasn't my own during pregnancy.

I won't lie; I became pretty depressed. Because my previous pregnancy had been so horrific, I went back to giving myself the blood thinner shots every day. Unable to push myself while exercising, I gave up on keeping my body healthy and gave in to the temptation to eat whatever I wanted. I had constant brain fog and anxiety as well as high blood pressure. And I felt so crappy and out of it that I felt like I was losing precious time with my toddler.

At the same time, I was pushing my hair line, which I'd created while living in our previous home, and training my academy students over Zoom calls. Garrett was still hosting a variety of virtual and in-person events for Wake Up Warrior. We were doing well financially, but making enough money to own our new home outright was a lot of pressure.

As with the first Strand house, we gained full ownership of our home within six months, but I didn't enjoy the achievement. I was sick from the pregnancy and sick with worry about my oldest.

Many times as parents, we have checklists for our kids: they should be in certain activities but not others; they should make great grades so they can go to excellent schools. But when Bailee was three, God flat out told me that she would have her own path, that I needed to keep her safe but let her go. So I tried not to set expectations for her life but instead leaned in to what she was interested in. This is probably one of the hardest things to do as a mom because you want to create the perfect path for your child, but the reality is that you don't know what the perfect path is.

When Bailee became a teenager, she became increasingly

messy, disrespectful, and reckless. I won't get into the specifics of the trouble she got into, but I started having nightmares that some late night, I would receive a phone call that my daughter was dead on the beach. I could see things spiraling, but there was no reasoning with her, no consequences that changed her behavior.

A few months into my already high-risk pregnancy, I couldn't handle the stress anymore. For a while, Garrett had been suggesting that we send Bailee to a wilderness camp in Utah, where kids were removed from technology and their peers. My sister-in-law had actually sent her oldest daughter to one and said she came back totally transformed. But it still broke my heart when my husband dropped my firstborn off.

As a mother, sometimes you have to make difficult decisions for your children, even if it means they'll be mad at you—even if they'll be mad at you for a long time. The stress of keeping Bailee safe while managing a high-risk pregnancy was too much for me to bear, but sending her away was still one of the hardest things I've ever done.

Oh my god, I thought when Bailee's first devastating letter from camp arrived. The kids weren't allowed to have phones, so she couldn't even call me. *What have I done?*

Of course, the camp counselors had warned us that reading Bailee's letters would be tough. Kids don't go to camp willingly, and they're often resentful for years. But I was super hormonal from the pregnancy and from being apart from my oldest. By the time I finished reading that first letter, I was sobbing.

It would've eased my mom guilt to keep Bailee close to me. As mothers, we often think we have to do everything, handle everything ourselves; otherwise, we're not doing our jobs. Sending my oldest away reminded me of how broken I felt when nursing her—how my nipples were always inflamed, how my milk never regulated, how it felt like my body had betrayed me when it came to the most basic of maternal functions. No one told me it was okay, that I could accept help.

Likewise, I felt broken sending Bailee to the wilderness. It was as if I'd failed at being her mother. And to be honest, I still sometimes feel guilty about the whole situation. Even though she now understands why it happened, to this day my daughter will occasionally talk about how painful that time was for her. But it was the right decision, and we both know it.

It's interesting because Garrett and I almost got two sets of the same kids. Bailee and Isla are creative and social but prone to anxiety and meltdowns; Ruby and Charlie are hardworking and quiet but can have an attitude. I did my best raising my older girls, but I was in my twenties. I didn't know that the worst thing you can do as a parent is be reactive, that yelling just makes your child either retreat or get defensive. I only wish that I had been as patient and empathetic with my older girls as I now am with my younger ones.

After three months at wilderness camp, Bailee went to a boarding school, which was recommended by the counselors as a transition back to normal life. There, she was allowed to call us once a week as well as use an iPod, go on walks, and work out at the gym. She was doing better and understood our decision to send her away, even if she still felt angry about it.

Bailee finally returned home about a month before my youngest was born, and I was so relieved to have her back. All I wanted then was to continue doing my job as a mother: keeping all my girls safe.

Around Thanksgiving, almost two full months before my baby was due, I went to the hospital with premature contractions and high blood pressure. Afterward, I was in and out of the hospital and my doctor's office, wondering how my baby and I would possibly make it to the end of January.

Once it became clear that I wasn't going to make it to full

term, my doctor decided to give me a daily steroid that would help develop my baby's lungs, since preemies often struggle with breathing. I just hoped she wouldn't come on Christmas Day, if only because my doctor was going out of town. But I somehow doubted she'd wait even that long.

One night, around 11:00 p.m., I was sitting in bed when I started seeing stars and feeling like I might black out. Garrett was in another room with our kids, so I stood to get him—then fell onto the floor. I began crawling toward the door, calling his name.

When he found me, Garrett took my blood pressure and sent it to my doctor. He immediately called us, saying, "Her blood pressure is stroke-level high, and you need to get to the hospital right now."

So we called Parker, who was now twenty-one and living on his own, and he and his girlfriend came over to watch our kids. Garrett then hurried me to the hospital, where I was given something to get my heart rate and blood pressure down.

"Right now, we're going to stabilize you," a doctor said, "and in the morning, we'll most likely induce. But maybe not."

Are you fucking kidding me? I thought.

"Absolutely not," I replied out loud. "You guys have sent me home like this several times now. I'm not leaving until this baby is born."

The overnight doctor didn't appreciate that, but in the morning, another doctor came and looked at my chart. "These numbers are out of control," he said. "We need to induce."

Thank God.

Because I'd had such a horrible experience with my third daughter's birth, I told my delivery team that I wanted as many pain meds as they could give me—"Just drug me up. I want to sleep through this delivery"—which is funny because I normally prefer to do things more naturally.

I gotta say, though, my last delivery was by far my easiest. I was loopy, but I wasn't in pain as I slept and watched movies. It was great.

Eventually, my doctor came in to check on me and said I was ready to go. I pushed one time, and my darling Charlie popped right out. She was tiny—just barely over five pounds—but healthy. "She's little but strong," one nurse commented.

Unfortunately, Charlie was extremely colicky for a couple of months, and I had severe postpartum depression. I didn't take medication because I knew it would pass, but I couldn't care less about work. I couldn't be bothered to do much at all, even though I didn't feel comfortable in my skin or my head. It wasn't until Garrett hired a night nanny and I got some sleep that I began to feel normal.

But, of course, that sense of normalcy didn't last.

Once again, after having my baby, everybody told me not to be hard on myself. "You're older. It's going to take longer to lose the weight." But I now knew how to exercise and diet in a healthy way; I wanted to see if I could be disciplined enough to get fit in record time.

That being said, I definitely put too much pressure on myself to be picture perfect, whether that meant losing baby weight or scaling my business. When someone tells me not to do something for whatever reason, my reaction is *I'll show you*. But this sometimes causes unrealistic, self-imposed expectations. It sometimes makes me feel like nothing is ever good enough.

Men don't usually think, *I have to spend half my day with my kids. I have to drop a couple of sizes.* They can simply be providers, while women are expected by society to wear multiple hats—to be moms and boss babes and hot girls—yet those external expectations aren't enough. We often add to our own stress with self-induced pressure to be achievers and performers. And for what?

If you're like this, try to take a step back and ask yourself if what you're currently doing is healthy. Perhaps, in this season, you need to show up more as a wife. Perhaps you need to focus on how you're responding to your kids. Perhaps you need to level up in your career. You can give some time and energy to each area of your life, but pushing yourself in every area all at once will only lead to burnout.

Admittedly, I'm not good at having the clarity to conserve my finite energy—or spread it around. In three months, I lost all fifty-five pounds of the pregnancy weight I'd gained. I then started weight lifting to regain all the muscle I'd lost. Then, after I quit nursing, I had a boob job done.

I'd had my first breast augmentation when I was eighteen—it was a trend at the time—but I had always felt self-conscious about how high the implants were. After Ruby was born, I got another one to correct the previous procedure, thinking I wouldn't have any more issues since I was probably done having kids. But now I'd nursed four babies, and my boobs were absolutely ruined. So I researched the best cosmetic doctors in Orange County and scheduled the procedure with enough time to recover and train for a third bikini competition.

I might've been grouchy from going so hard with diet and exercise, but I remember that competition as being great. With my family complete and my body back, I stepped onto the stage more confident than ever and won best overall, even though I was five feet three and thirty-nine years old—even though I was standing next to an actual Barbie doll, a woman who was about six feet tall and had gorgeous blonde locks.

Later, when I said how I just couldn't believe it, my trainer shrugged. "You have better symmetry."

But as all this was happening, my homelife was becoming more and more chaotic. In addition to the night nanny, Garrett said we should hire a second daytime nanny. There had been multiple instances, like the night before Charlie was born, when our regular nanny wasn't available. "Who knows what we would've done if Parker hadn't been around?" he said. He didn't want to be left in a precarious situation like that again.

At the same time, we had homeschool teachers for Bailee and Ruby, a holdover from the COVID-19 shutdowns. Ruby loved her teacher and thrived in a homeschool environment, but Bailee hated hers and refused to get out of bed to learn. I told her she couldn't do nothing and sent her to the local public school, thinking she'd at least have some structure.

Finally, Garrett hired a home manager to coordinate projects around our twelve-thousand-square-foot home. The problem was that the home manager was just a kid—one who cost us $10,000 when we asked him to change the front and back locks and he replaced every single lock in our giant house. Nobody was really managing the home, and things were spiraling.

Being pregnant and postpartum can sometimes feel dehumanizing because people—in trying to protect you—think you can't do anything. During my pregnancy, I'd stepped back from work to focus on my family, and now my salon was basically running itself. Then Garrett had hired a home manager, two homeschool teachers, and three nannies, so now I had several people in my home at all times of the day that I had to coordinate—and therefore spent less time with my girls.

At a certain level, I understood that all the people in my home and at my salon were trying to protect me by taking on my responsibilities. But it made me feel incapable. Like, *Am I really that out of it? Am I really doing that badly?*

I also realized that sometimes adding more people doesn't fix anything; it only creates more chaos. During that period, I became so overwhelmed and claustrophobic that I no longer enjoyed the big, beautiful house that my husband and I worked so hard for. Worse yet, in handing over most of my responsibilities as a mother and entrepreneur, I entirely lost my sense of purpose.

I could tell the pressure of our enlarged life was weighing on Garrett as well. At various points in our marriage, he'd dull his stress with alcohol, but currently, he was addicted to a tonic called Feel Free, which is supposed to help with relaxation and productivity. It was fine when he was having the recommended maximum of one each day, but then he started having two. Then three. We were still having weekly date nights, recording our podcast, and taking family trips, but his eyes were always bloodshot. I could tell he was checked out, numb.

Garrett saw that taking the tonic was a problem and tried to stop cold turkey on a trip to Cabo, but he relapsed multiple times over the course of a year. I tried to help him as much as I could, but we weren't connecting. As a result, any support I offered came across as criticism.

This was a scary, vulnerable place for me because I didn't want to risk my or my girls' financial security, but I knew Garrett and I would naturally drift apart if something didn't change. And after fighting for our marriage for so many years, I really didn't want to lose him.

Yet Feel Free wasn't the only splinter in our relationship. Garrett became reckless with money too, spending hundreds of thousands of dollars flying private just because he could. I'll admit I liked flying private for a couple of family vacations, but there was no reason to do so every time he had a business trip.

Eventually, Garrett realized that he didn't want to say goodbye to his family just to continue grinding. He kicked the Feel Free addiction and became more fiscally responsible, and together, we let go of some of the people needlessly occupying our home. We were literally and figuratively cleaning house.

Like our early marriage, this period was a reminder that there's a dark side to success. The desire to check certain boxes (e.g., businesses worth billions, sprawling mansions, luxury cars, model-thin bodies) leads to you always looking for the next big thing. It leads to dissatisfaction in the present and anxiety for the future.

In our second house in the Strand, Garrett and I remembered that we had so much to be grateful for. We remembered that obstacles are put in your path to prepare you for who you're meant to become. But I had a creeping feeling that we weren't in the clear yet.

Bailee hated public school even more than her homeschool teacher, and honestly, I couldn't blame her. Her high school, Dana Hills, had such a bad reputation that it was called "Dana Pills." My daughter often complained about kids being drunk and high, but the truth of what she was facing hit hard one afternoon when she sent me a photo of a Jack Daniel's bottle in a toilet. I couldn't keep her there but didn't know what else to do; after she'd spent time at a wilderness camp and boarding school, the private schools nearby wouldn't take her.

This was a difficult period for me because, as mentioned, I was juggling having a newborn, a toddler, and two teenagers. How could I inspire Bailee without controlling her, especially while also caring for my other girls? I knew my oldest was depressed, but like most people, I believed getting a high school diploma or GED was the bare minimum.

A few days after sending me the photo of the waterlogged Jack Daniel's bottle, Bailee asked to attend a two-day music camp in Costa Mesa. I didn't think much of it, other than that it would be nice for her to spend time with other artists. After all, my daughter had been in several school plays over the years, had an incredible singing voice, had taught herself guitar, and was a gifted songwriter. I had no idea that camp would change everything.

The day I dropped her off, Bailee was wearing a lace shirt with chains across it, hot pink cheetah pants, and chunky, Bratz-style platforms. It was so quirky that I felt like I was seeing her personality come back. And wouldn't you know it? She fit right in with the other kids at the camp.

But when I picked her up, Bailee said, "Mom, the owner wants to talk to you."

Oh no.

"About what?" I asked.

"I don't know."

Of course that had me worried, but when I spoke to the owner, he told me how impressed he was with Bailee. He said that he wanted to work with her, help her hone her natural talent so that she could pursue music as a career. He wanted to work with her every day if possible.

That's when I felt a familiar nudge, the one that said to take the unfamiliar path. If Bailee was going to pursue music, why wait until after high school? What did she really need a GED for? She could always get one later if she wanted to. My parents—most parents, for that matter—would've never let that fly, but as long as she wasn't staying in bed all day, as long as she was actively pursuing her passion, then I was content.

So the camp owner, Bailee, and I worked out a plan for her to study music in lieu of attending high school. Some days, she would learn about songwriting. Others, production or content creation. Her days were as long as regular school days; she just wasn't in a traditional school.

I won't say this was the best part, but I did love when people would ask where Bailee went to school and I'd reply, "Oh, she dropped out." I'd laugh at their shocked expressions, then explain how she was preparing for a music career. Most people were curious about how that worked, which led to conversations about leaning in to your children's passions instead of making them do the things that you think they should. Furthermore, Bailee's unique schooling proved what God had told me when she was three years old: she would have her own path.

I'm not saying, of course, that everyone should let their kids drop out. Even hair school requires you to have a GED. What I am saying is that some people's paths diverge early in life; as parents, we should be aware of the paths that best suit our specific children—and create new ones when needed.

After hearing about Bailee, people were, unsurprisingly, curious about what my other teenager, Ruby, was up to, but those girls are polar opposites. While my oldest is messy, my second-born daughter has been making her bed and doing her own laundry since she was twelve. Even with friends, she has a hard time getting out of her comfort zone or saying what she's feeling. She's levelheaded and hates drama. In other words, she's a lot like me (apart from the cleanliness thing).

Ruby hasn't expressed a particular career interest yet, but I believe she'll find a path that's well suited to her wit and charm. It might just take longer for her than for some people, like it did for me. (In high school, my mom was concerned about me because my grades weren't great, I didn't have any passions, and I wasn't ambitious. I didn't know what to do with my life and really only went into hair by default...but look at what I've created using the tool of doing hair.)

People tell me all the time, "But I'm just a mom. I don't have a passion. How can I build a business?" So I want to share that sometimes people find their path, their purpose, only *after* leveraging their existing skills. Everyone, including a stay-at-home mom, has skills they've picked up along the way. The trick is monetizing them.

Take my younger sister as an example. A stay-at-home mom

who struggled for years with an eating disorder, she recently started making these protein bites that taste like Crumbl cookies. It was just a healthy treat meant to solve the problem she was personally facing, but at a party, friends started asking for the recipe. That's when she realized that she could build a business.

My sister is still in the beginning stages of launching Cait's Fit Bites, but already I can see the impact that her sharing her story and her treats will have on women. It's a joy to help her grow, to encourage her in hiring an assistant and creating a website—in turning her struggles into purpose.

All of that is to say, sometimes passion drives success, like it did for Bailee. But often, skills drive success, which drives passion, which drives purpose. For instance, I wasn't passionate about hair when I started, but seeing how I was developing a following *and* positively impacting women kindled a newfound love for the art of styling hair. In turn, that love led to me wanting to improve my skills and teach others.

I'm telling you this because I wish someone had told me that it's awesome to know exactly what you want to do at an early age, but it's not necessary. It's okay to figure it out while gaining life experience. Just open yourself up to possibilities, allow yourself to try them out, and be willing to change.

In 2023, Garrett and I started attending business events in Miami, and I loved the energy of the city. I thought we might buy a second home there someday or move after all the kids were older. Yet every time I think something will happen in ten years, it happens much sooner.

In the meantime, I was struck by the numbers people were sharing at these events. Some of them were making as much in a month as I did in a year, and it was humbling. I wondered, *Why can't I 10x my business?*

But I knew why. For a couple of years, I'd been ignoring my

top stylist's problematic behavior. I brushed it off when she made snide remarks about me being two minutes late to record my own podcast. I assumed that she had a good reason when she randomly kicked students out of my online academy and offered them refunds. I tolerated the way she spoke to me and the rest of my team because she was running the show; I thought that I would have to go back to working full-time if I fired her.

People always ask me how I balance everything, but the truth is I don't. During some seasons, I put most of my time and energy into my marriage and kids, and during others, I put most of it into my business. With my high-risk pregnancy, my oldest's concerning behavior, my husband's checked-out state, and so on, I'd chosen during that period to put everything I had into supporting my family and my health. But that meant I was willfully looking past the red flags at my salon.

I want to emphasize here that I absolutely could have supported both my household and my work. Mom guilt was telling me that I needed to just be with my kids, that I needed to let my business go, but I could've put a little more of my time and energy into the team managing my salon. If I had, I might not have made the same mistake I'd made with my first team: choosing friendship over communication.

This time, that mistake was not made because I didn't know better; it was made to keep the peace, to make my life a little easier. But the result was the same. My top stylist had lost sight of the vision for my brand, and now her attitude was infecting the rest of the team.

Why am I letting her hold my business hostage? I asked myself at one business event in Miami. I thought about how I had trained her to connect with students through her story but how she now sounded scripted. It felt dirty rather than inspiring. *Why am I letting her turn my message into something superficial?*

After returning home, I asked this stylist to come into my office. She knew what was happening; as I said, ever since losing my first team, I'd done my own firing. It was scary at first, but I believe that I owe it to people to look them in the eye and say, "Hey, this is no longer working."

"I love you," I said, and it was true. We'd grown close in the aftermath of losing my first team, as well as through the podcast and live events. But although I considered us friends, I knew the negative impact she was having on my team and hair community. I could see the red flags I'd ignored for two years while trying to survive the chaos of my homelife.

I also knew that if something is not working, as a business owner, you have to make tough choices regardless of friendship. "It's just," I continued, "I don't think you actually want to be here anymore. I wish you the best."

She teared up and hugged me, but when I asked if she needed anything, I saw her fake smile slide into place. "No, that's okay," she said with no real emotion.

Wow, thank you for making that so easy for me, I thought.

I did truly care for this stylist, but by that point, everything she did felt manipulative. She'd positioned herself as the queen of the salon, so it was a power struggle whenever I stepped in as the boss. I could no longer tolerate that, so I had to let her go.

I'll admit there was some backlash. Like with my first salon walkout, letting go of my top stylist caused a divide among my team, clients, and students. But this time, my community included almost five hundred artists. The divide had a direct impact on my community and resulted in financial loss for my business, so I had to cut the cancer before it continued to spread.

What's especially crazy is that my remaining team and I didn't take on much more extra work after that stylist left. According to them, she would come in for a couple of hours in the morning, then go home to work on her own projects. My story had been that I couldn't fire her because I would have to return to work full-time, but I found that I had almost as much time for my family as I did before.

Be careful of the stories you tell yourself. They can shape your reality, so you need to learn which you should lean in to and which you should let go.

While all the drama with my salon was going on, I kept thinking about Miami. Garrett and I had worked so hard to buy our house that I thought it would be in our family forever, but we weren't happy there. It was way too much, practically a symbol of the toll success can take.

That's when I had a vision of a home near the coast, with a view of the city skyline and fireworks going off nearby. I realized, *This isn't my house; it's God's house. He simply gave us the opportunity to get here through faith and hard work. If He can do that, what else might He do in our lives?*

The following night, when we were on a date at a restaurant called Coastal Kitchen, I told Garrett, "Let's put the house up for sale."

We locked eyes, and I could tell without a word that he was also ready to go. He pulled out his phone and texted our Realtor, and within a few months, we'd found a home in Miami, finished touch-ups in our current house, and gotten an offer on it. The whole process was quicker than I could've imagined.

Despite the drama with my top stylist, my salon was not crumbling. It wasn't my most profitable endeavor, but it practically ran itself, so I didn't see any point in letting it go when we moved. I also didn't want to put people out of work, so I figured I'd just manage the salon remotely, maybe fly in a couple of times each month.

However, as Garrett and I were preparing for the move, it

became obvious that my former top stylist's bad behavior had rubbed off on the rest of the team. Have you ever walked into a room only for it to get quiet, like everybody was just talking shit about you? That's how team meetings were starting to feel.

If I'm being honest, I didn't truly know every detail of my business because I had stepped out for a couple of years, but I was starting to wonder if my team was only there for job security. Content decisions were being made behind my back, and much of that content seemed like it was being made so that it could later be repurposed. Any input I gave was laughed at, then they would say things to try and appease me. Everyone was obviously exhausted and overworked, yet the business's numbers were declining. I got the sense that the team seemed out of capacity because they were keeping their jobs and building their own brands.

During that period, I had crucial conversations with several stylists about how they were clearly only remaining because they were salaried. They weren't interested in my vision for propelling the business forward. I didn't fault them for wanting to support their families, but I kept hearing how tired they were when the salon wasn't seeing results. It didn't add up. I knew they were there just to collect their paychecks, yet they kept assuring me that they were there for *me*.

Assurances aside, I could tell that I was being pushed out of my own business. When I would come into the salon with one of my crazy, visionary ideas, the manager would say, "It's a great idea, but you don't know the trickle effect it would have on us. We're already going in a different direction, and that would completely derail everything."

Because I wasn't the one who would implement the idea, I felt I couldn't argue. As long as the salon was profitable, I wouldn't micromanage day-to-day operations. But the numbers kept declining until the salon had its first year where it lost money.

Around the same time, God was telling me to reach outside the hair community, that I had more to share with a wider audience. It'd been a long time since I'd regularly stood behind a chair, yet letting go of the identity *stylist* was scary because hair was the trade I'd built my business on—like a restaurant franchise owner who thought of themselves as the one flipping burgers. After all these years, I still suffered from imposter syndrome, so the last thing I wanted was to feel like a dummy in the personal development space.

But I'd outgrown my niche. I had credibility that could be leveraged to support women who were raising families and building businesses. So I decided to return to how it all started: as a highly personal brand. After all, what initially drove sales when I had nothing but my name was my authenticity and vulnerability.

I thought the best way to begin rebranding was to tell my team to change the name of *Big Money Stylist* to *The Danielle K. White Show*. The podcast's focus on hair was making it stagnant, and I felt like my heart was no longer in it. So I would launch my rebrand with an episode I'd recorded with a big-name influencer outside the hair industry. I made it clear that this idea was not up for negotiation.

That's when I realized just how much I had lost control of my business, just how little my team respected me and my vision. The next day, when I asked if my episode had gone up, a team member sent me a link to Spotify, and I saw that they'd posted it on a brand-new channel with zero views or downloads. Did they think I was too stupid to notice? To add insult to injury, I also saw that they posted an episode that *they'd* recorded about hair on the channel for *Big Money Stylist*.

The betrayal I felt then was greater than even the first salon walkout because it was incredibly disrespectful. I rebranded in an effort to get more exposure—why would they sabotage that?

What they did was embarrassing, and I saw how they truly didn't care what I said. Now that the salon was no longer profitable and most of the team was only there for job security, what was the point of keeping the doors open?

When I brought up their blatant disregard of my wishes, my team was dead silent. Then, when I prompted them for a reason, they admitted that they were preparing for the salon to close. Were they trying to position themselves as the face of my brand? Why were they so tired when numbers were continually declining? It was clear they were creating an exit plan.

This was yet another example of how I failed to communicate during that period. I'd had no intention of closing the salon, yet my team members assumed that I would, and their scarcity mindsets led to them acting in their own best interests. Their behavior was unacceptable, but the situation could've been less ugly if I had been more aware.

I did ultimately decide to close the salon. I'd leaned on my team when I was taking care of my kids and health, thinking I could come back to take care of any little fires that popped up, but by the time I returned, I was too late. The fire was all-consuming, and I had to let it burn itself out.

I regret how the closure happened, but I found that losing most of that team and the staff at my house was liberating. After dropping all that dead weight, I had the exciting and terrifying chance to do something bigger and better without the input of people who didn't support my vision.

I realized then that sometimes we get stuck in a business or with people when growth isn't happening because we don't want to mess with the status quo. But we can't move on if we're shackled to the present. We have to let go to get through.

Interestingly, the people who chose to stick by my side, whose drive and heart aligned with mine, are all the most successful and generous people from my team. People like my nanny, who loves my girls wholeheartedly. A few of my stylists/trainers, who have all now built their own salons. My personal assistant and social media manager, who have taken my brand to new heights through their ingenious strategies. These were the people who cared about connecting with and making an impact on others. The ones who I wanted to work with during my next chapter.

I thought back to that night in the hot tub, when my life felt perfect. *If I asked you to go again, would you?*

My life felt far from perfect now, but it also felt full of promise. *Yes,* I answered once more. *Absolutely.*

CONCLUSION

"I THINK THE FRANCHISE IDEA IS A DISTRACTION RIGHT now," a business coach told me shortly after Garrett and I moved our family to Miami.

I was surprised, but I'd reached out to him to brainstorm options for scaling my business. I wasn't going to dismiss his opinion out of hand. "What do you mean?" I asked.

He talked about how there were tons of hairstylists now who were doing beautiful work. And as I well knew, many of them used techniques similar to mine—or even derived from mine. Before duplicating my business, I needed to distinguish myself from the current competition.

That was a light bulb moment for me. As mentioned, I'd been hearing God tell me to make my business more personal and less industry-specific, but I didn't know how or why. All that I knew was that this transition would start with rebranding my podcast *Big Money Stylist* as *The Danielle K. White Show*. But branching out as Danielle seemed scary when I'd only ever really interviewed and supported hairstylists.

Talking with that business coach, however, I remembered that it wasn't my hair skills that had connected with people in the beginning; it was my authenticity and vulnerability. I needed to return to my early messaging, before it was diluted by my team's voices, so that I could build stronger connections. These connections would not only allow me to scale my business, but they would also enable me to empower women from all walks of life.

We as a society are undoubtedly about to face a massive transition. Given how easy it is to rent an exotic vehicle for Instagram reels or even generate fake videos with AI, I predict that people will have an even greater desire to seek out authentic and vulnerable creators and brands. Trust is key in relationships, and relationships are key in business.

Unlike in 2008, when Garrett and I ignored the signs of coming change, we'll adjust accordingly, and I hope you will too. I hope you will make scary moves based on what your intuition or God is telling you, knowing you'll be prepared when the world catches up. Remember, opportunities often open up only *after* you've shown the faith and willingness to pivot.

In writing this book, I realized that I would like to support women one-on-one, so I launched a coaching program. My imposter syndrome told me that I wasn't qualified, but Garrett reminded me that I have more hands-on experience as a parent and entrepreneur than most in the coaching space. Many of them have theoretical knowledge, given that they don't have kids, partners, and/or successful businesses. I'm qualified, I have to remind myself, *because of* all the lessons I've learned living.

Plus, I now have valuable coaching experience from leading couples' events with my husband. Around the time that we moved to Miami, our podcast *Date Your Wife* gained serious momentum—to the point where we were being stopped in airports. People were asking us to start coaching, and with our relationship more solid than ever, we decided to give it a shot. I'm pleased to say that it's going well so far.

As of right now, I'm continuing to teach because NBR has one of the most sought-after extension courses out there. I'm also expanding my hair line to more products. Maybe eventually I will start a salon franchise, as I originally thought. Or maybe I'll host smaller, more intimate events aimed at lifting up all women, whether they're hairstylists or not. Regardless, I'm excited to see where God leads me next.

I tell you all this because it's easy to get so caught up in arriving at a specific destination that you forget the journey never ends—in business and relationships alike. You don't live happily ever after when you make a million dollars, just as you don't die when you lose it all. There's always a new path to explore, and along the way, you'll inevitably discover more about yourself that you like and more that you'd like to change.

These days, Garrett and I are both learning that success doesn't have to be a solo endeavor; in fact, your perceived competition can be your best collaborators. That's why I started inviting big names from a variety of fields on *The Danielle K. White Show*, even though for years I feared being rejected by those same people. That's why Garrett and another influential men's coach coordinated a tour called The Man in the Arena, which has already gained massive momentum in the men's personal development space.

In between our professional pursuits, Garrett and I are soaking in time with our family as well as celebrating their accomplishments. Parker, who also moved to Miami and is currently Garrett's top sales agent, recently got engaged. Bailee just moved into her own apartment and is working for me while pursuing her music career. Ruby took the cross-country move a bit harder but is making new friends and discovering new interests. And my little ones, Isla and Charlie, are as cute as ever yet becoming more self-sufficient every day.

That's not to say everything is picture perfect now. The White household is a constant zoo, an absolute shit show. With toddlers and teenagers running around, their emotions all over the place, Garrett and I often wonder, *Why in the hell did we do this to ourselves?* We're still in the thick of the chaotic years, but we wouldn't have it any other way.

It feels a bit weird rebranding while raising two young girls, just as I once built my brand while raising their older sisters. It's almost like déjà vu. But I'm fortunate to have perspective now, to know that the work will be worthwhile, that if I'm willing to do the work, a plan will be revealed, and a door will open.

Not long ago, a couple that I was scared to invite onto my podcast made a point of telling me that they built their business and strengthened their marriage after hearing Garrett and me share our story. The lives they've changed were due, in part, to us having the courage to do things differently. Even when others didn't get it. Even when we didn't like each other. Even when we wanted to quit. Even when success was taking its toll.

That conversation really underscored the impact we've had, so I want to leave you with this: whether you call it God or intuition, you have a voice, a knowing within you that you can tap into, just like I have. You have the power to not only change your life for the better, but also to positively impact so many others. Just listen, and then act.

ACKNOWLEDGMENTS

THIS BOOK IS A REFLECTION OF THE LAST DECADE OF MY life—building a brand, building a marriage, raising children, and becoming the woman I was always meant to be. None of this was done alone.

First, I acknowledge my husband. Thank you for seeing more in me than I could see in myself, for pushing me when I wanted to retreat, for guiding me when I felt unsure, and for leading our family with strength, vision, and love. Your belief in me has been a constant anchor through every season of growth.

To my children—you are my highest purpose. You have shaped my priorities, softened my heart, and given meaning to the work I do and the woman I strive to become. Everything I build is with you in mind.

And above all, I acknowledge my faith. The quiet, steady whisper that has guided me when the path was unclear. The voice that has led me, corrected me, and reminded me to trust even when I didn't understand the next step. This book exists because I leaned in to that guidance and allowed it to write through me.

To everyone who finds themselves within these pages, I hope my journey reminds you that you are never walking alone—and that when you listen closely, you may discover that God is writing your story too.